CLASSROOM DYNAMICS

CLASSROOM DYNAMICS

Practical Strategies for Dealing with Off-Task Behaviour

GLEN PEARSALL

To Noah and Jem, who during homeschooling over the long Melbourne lockdown made sure that I continued to refine my skills for dealing with challenging behaviour.

Note: All student names and details have been changed. Composite examples have also been used to preserve student anonymity.

© Glen Pearsall 2024

First published in 2021 by Hawker Brownlow Education
This updated edition published in 2024 by Amba Press

All rights reserved. No part of this book may be reproduced or transmitted in any form or by any means, electronic or mechanical, including photocopying, recording or by any information storage and retrieval system, without prior permission in writing from the publisher.

Published by Amba Press
Melbourne, Australia
www.ambapress.com.au

ISBN: 9781923116498 (pbk)
ISBN: 9781923116504 (ebk)

A catalogue record for this book is available from the National Library of Australia.

Contents

Acknowledgements ix
Introduction 1

Part 1: Practical strategies for dealing with off-task behaviour **9**
Chapter 1 Low-key interventions 11
Chapter 2 Giving explicit instructions 25
Chapter 3 Low-demand instruction 37
Chapter 4 Pivoting 51
Chapter 5 Talking it out 61
Chapter 6 Seeking support 79

Part 2: Understanding entrenched off-task behaviour **85**
Chapter 7 What is the purpose of off-task behaviour? 87
Chapter 8 Tailoring interventions for individual student needs 97

Part 3: Avoiding off-task behaviour **101**
Chapter 9 Transitions and procedures 103
Chapter 10 Establishing student engagement 115
Chapter 11 Enhancing student engagement 131

Conclusion 147
Appendix: Break glass in case of emergency learning games 151
About the author 163
References 165
Index 169

Acknowledgements

Thanks to the teachers – those I worked with and those who taught me – who inspired many of the strategies in this book. I want to particularly extend my appreciation to those teachers who took part in video coaching with me or invited me into their classrooms, often in challenging situations when they were at their most vulnerable. You have helped ensure that the strategies in this book are as practical and effective as possible. I have not used your names in these pages, but you will recognise your persistence and professionalism throughout.

And, of course, thank you to all the students who I have worked with, many of whom were more than eager to give me feedback on my performance ...

Introduction

In my second semester of teaching, I started an argument with a student by simply asking him to close a door he had just passed through.

'Why do I have to?' was his immediate response.

'There's a wasp nest over there and I don't want them to end up in the classroom.'

The student protested that wasn't his responsibility: 'I didn't open it.'

I pointed out to him that he did use the doorway though, and was in fact the last one through it, so could he please close it?

'No,' he replied, 'I don't think even wasps would want to come to this class – they find it so boring.' This got a ripple of laughter from the students seated near the door leading him to repeat his comment louder. He added a couple of other reasons why a wasp would find my class unappealing. By now every student in the room was listening and this seemed to give him confidence in his defiance: 'I am not wasting my time getting up and going all the way over to close the door when the wasps aren't even going to come in!'

I took the bait and got dragged into a long back and forth about whether or not wasps were likely to enter the classroom through an open door. Finally, exasperated, I pointed out to him that while we had been talking two wasps had indeed flown into the room.

'I know, that's why I left it open – so we could let the wasps out.'

I had absolutely no idea what to say to that. My teacher training hadn't exactly prepared me for a situation like this. Indeed, while we covered educational theory, curriculum delivery and general principles of building a positive classroom, all the nuances of instructional practice were not something I had studied. I had to develop my toolkit for dealing with off-task behaviour through trial and error.

There was a lot of error.

Of course, there is nothing wrong with this. Good learning is not about avoiding mistakes. It is rather about making *high-quality* mistakes. Instead of making the same errors over and over again, you want to make new errors. You want to find new gaps in your practice, stumble as you try new things and use this as feedback to constantly refine what you are doing.

As with most teachers I know, it was my colleagues who helped me most in this process. The teachers I worked with gave me lots of practical strategies for keeping my classes positive and engaged. Much of the best advice didn't come from formal training but through quick chats at the photocopier or debriefing about a challenging class at the lunchroom table. What stood out about this advice was that it was so practical: small, concrete adjustments to my teaching that I could put into action immediately.

However, the problem with this process of trial and error is that it is so time intensive. It can take years to build up a toolkit of strategies for addressing all the complexities of the behavioural issues you encounter in the classroom – and even longer to practise and refine their execution so that they suit you and your school setting. Moreover, this time-consuming process doesn't ever really end; experienced teachers will often encounter a student or a whole class that has them reviewing their technique all over again.

Unfortunately, time is usually what most teachers lack. Teachers are notoriously time-poor, often working many more hours than they are paid, with new responsibilities being added to the role seemingly every year. This lack of time often leads to the paradoxical situation where the urgent demands of the everyday classroom swamp the important work of learning how to reduce these urgent demands. It is hard to do a deep dive into the research around dealing with off-task behaviour when you are trying to deal with and follow up on the consequences of the off-task behaviour in your class.

This can be emotionally taxing. It might be reassuring to know that, in the long run, you will master ways to de-escalate emotional outbursts from students. However, that doesn't always make it less stressful in the moment – or any less embarrassing that they can be heard in the classroom next door through the thin partition wall.

Classroom Dynamics has been written to address this issue. It has been designed to accelerate the process of building up an effective toolkit for creating and maintaining positive classrooms. Echoing my mentor teachers' advice to me, it offers you concrete tips that can be implemented *immediately* with your students. Moreover, it is designed as a single volume resource that you can use to survey the best research about how to create engaged and independent learners so that you can quickly get to the heart of issues that might be affecting your students' learning.

This emphasis on practical quick-to-learn and apply strategies is reflected in the book's structure.

How to use this text

Part 1: Practical strategies for dealing with off-task behaviour

If you are having difficulty managing a student, group of students or even an entire class's behaviour, start here. This section explores a series of practical responses to students who are 'off task'. They are loosely organised according to the intensity of the teacher intervention required to implement them, from subtle low-key reminders to more overt directives, to (the often time-intensive) strategies for addressing student resistance, resolving conflict and establishing a whole-school response to these behaviours.

- In **Chapter 1: Low-key interventions** we focus on quick techniques for subtly encouraging students back on task.
- In **Chapter 2: Giving explicit instructions** we explore the use of brief verbal interventions for reminding students of your expectations.
- In **Chapter 3: Low-demand instruction** we discuss how to use declarative language to give directions to students who are demand-avoidant.
- In **Chapter 4: Pivoting** we dive deeper into scripts for avoiding arguments and redirecting students back to their learning.
- In **Chapter 5: Talking it out** we discuss strategies for resolving emerging issues and de-escalating conflict.
- In **Chapter 6: Seeking support** we focus on advice on how to effectively elicit support from colleagues and school leaders.

For new teachers, this section offers a detailed road map for how to steer students back to their learning with as little fuss as possible. For more experienced teachers, these chapters might serve as a reminder of overlooked strategies or subtle refinements you can make to established techniques.

Part 2: Understanding entrenched off-task behaviour

No strategy works in every situation. You need to develop ways to understand and respond to deep-seated behavioural issues that are hard to shift. If the strategies featured in Part 1 of this resource are ineffective, you need to look deeper at what is driving this entrenched behaviour. This section offers ways to both get a better sense of what might be driving the challenging behaviour of specific students and how to tailor an individual response to these needs.

- In **Chapter 7: What is the purpose of off-task behaviour?** we delve into the use of functional behaviour analysis to better understand and respond to patterns of challenging and 'rusted on' behaviours.
- In **Chapter 8: Tailoring interventions for individual student needs** we will walk through how to differentiate interventions for students who generally *can't* rather than *won't* behave appropriately.

Part 3: Avoiding off-task behaviour

The best way to deal with off-task behaviour is to stop it occurring in the first place. Inevitably, the sections of this book that explore strategies are somewhat reactive – they essay what to do when off-task behaviour takes place.

However, this section goes back a step and asks you to consider what you can do to avoid having to implement these strategies at all. It opens with a discussion of classroom procedures you can employ to ensure your classroom is an orderly space for learning. It then explores what are the underlying factors that drive student engagement and what you can do to enhance and maintain this engagement.

- In **Chapter 9: Transitions and procedures** we discuss how to establish routines to set high expectations and minimise disruptions.
- In **Chapter 10: Establishing student engagement** we explore how students need lessons that offers challenge, choice and purpose.
- In **Chapter 11: Enhancing student engagement** we identify strategies for maintaining and maximising engagement by building relationships, sparking curiosity and establishing a culture of feedback.

Adapting these strategies in your school

You should take careful note of how this approach is designed to fit within your school's established protocols around dealing with off-task behaviour:

most schools have clear procedures and policies for dealing with student behaviour. These differ widely from school to school. Your school might take a restorative justice approach, have a well-established positive behaviour framework or a clear list of expectations – and consequences for when these expectations are not met. The approach we discuss here is not an alternative to these well-established policies but rather a set of strategies for realising them in the everyday.

> The best way to deal with off-task behaviour is to stop it occurring in the first place.

This approach offers you subtle ways to reiterate the positive expectations behind these policy frameworks in your classroom. It explores techniques for reducing the frequency with which you have to rely on the school-level responses built into these documents for dealing with serious off-task behaviour. This focus on tactics and technique at the classroom level ensures that – regardless of what broader framework your school employs – the material covered here will have practical application with your students.

DEVELOPING AN EFFECTIVE APPROACH

Of course, being an effective classroom teacher is not just about having a toolkit of strategies but also having the right approach. Those colleagues who first gave me advice on how to deal with challenging classroom behaviour did more than offer me tips; they talked about and modelled the values that effective teachers bring to every encounter with a student.

The importance of having the right mindset is something I am constantly reminded of both as an educator and a teacher coach. Teachers who take the time to affirm and connect with their students and are proactive and strategic about how they go about doing this invariably get the most out of these strategies – and indeed their classes.

Throughout the wide-ranging discussion of teaching strategies in this book, we will return again and again to the principles that inform these techniques. This is sometimes done explicitly, but perhaps just as often it is implicit in the way I suggest implementing these techniques. I have listed these principles in the following pages to ensure that they are front of mind as you evaluate the strategies in this book – and in any encounter with your students.

Focus on building relationships

One of the golden rules of teaching is 'relationship first, task second'. Constantly looking for opportunities to connect with students makes it more likely you will meet them at their point of need and spend less time correcting off-task behaviour – and when you do have to address this behaviour students will be more likely to take up your advice.

Teach appropriate behaviour

Make explicit how you want students to behave. Don't presume they know what to do or get stuck insisting that they 'should know better'. Clearly describe your expectations and take on the responsibility for teaching them as you would for any other area of the curriculum. Students are more likely to be positive and successful learners when they know precisely what positive and successful learning looks like.

Be positive

When shaping classroom behaviour, what matters is often not what you say 'no' to but what you say 'yes' to. Endorse behaviour you want to see more of and tactically ignore, pivot around and de-escalate behaviours you want to minimise. 'Catching students behaving' in this way creates a positive classroom culture that allows all students to do their best.

> Make explicit how you want students to behave. Don't presume they know what to do or get stuck insisting 'they should know better.

Don't react, respond

When you encounter off-task behaviour, avoid emotional, first-impulse reactions that might escalate the situation. Instead, plan ahead. Anticipate common types of off-task behaviour and decide how you might best respond to them in a calm and considered manner. Having this bank of options then makes it easier to deal with issues quickly and confidently as they arise in the moment.

Address the behaviour – not the person

When you do have to correct a student's behaviour, make it clear that this is not personal. You are focussed on their actions, not them. This not only makes your interventions manageable in terms of scope – you are not trying to change who the student is but what they are doing – but also helps preserve your relationship. When the off-task behaviour ends, the point of contention between you disappears, and you get back to learning together.

Seek to understand

Reflect on what is driving a student's actions. Most off-task behaviour can be read as a kind of communication: what is this student's behaviour trying to tell you? Look to what happens immediately before and after an incident. If you can spot underlying patterns in a student's actions, you are much more likely to be able to help them – even if their behaviour is entrenched or particularly challenging.

> Most off-task behaviour can be read as a kind of communication: what is this student's behaviour trying to tell you?

Be strategic

Treat every incident of off-task behaviour as an opportunity to refine your technique. Avoid moral judgments – don't question the student's character or your own innate abilities – just focus on how well your strategy worked on this occasion and what you will try the next time you encounter this behaviour. A strategic approach like this helps give you emotional distance and a sense of agency – even in difficult or heated situations.

These principles empower your teaching. They ensure that no matter how challenging a class is, you feel like there is always something that you can try to address off-task behaviour. These principles remind you that while you may not be able to resolve every issue or find the right strategy every time, it is you who has the biggest say in what will happen. They remind you that the person you have the most influence over in the classroom is yourself.

Part 1
PRACTICAL STRATEGIES FOR DEALING WITH OFF-TASK BEHAVIOUR

Chapter 1
Low-key interventions

The very first lesson I observed as a student teacher was eye-opening. The lesson – a science class in a large suburban high school – began with a student loudly storming out of the classroom as the teacher was taking attendance. The student re-appeared a few minutes later at the open window of the room sitting on his bike. He stuck his arm through the window, grabbed the end of the hand towel from the dispenser over the sink and rode away still holding the hand towel as it trailed behind him, the roll spinning furiously in the dispenser. The class roared their appreciation. The lesson only deteriorated from there.

At the end of the session, I wasn't sure what to say to their teacher, so I mumbled something about it being a 'tough lesson' as I headed off to my next observation.

The teacher gave me a knowing smile. 'That was them on a *good* day.'

When teachers talk about the challenges of classroom management, they tend to focus on the most challenging episodes, the outlying behaviours. This is understandable. It is hard when discussing a particular behaviour management strategy not to think about whether that would really work with that 'tricky' student or with that 'difficult' class.

However, this can be a trap. Mastering how to deal with all the low-level off-task behaviours that distract students from their learning is an important everyday skill in its own right. Moreover, our capacity to deal with more extreme behaviours is often actually determined by whether we have the headspace and time to properly address these behaviours. Being able to quickly steer off-task students back to their learning without a great deal of effort means you can devote your energies to teaching and learning – and if a more serious issue does arise you can concentrate your full attention to resolving it.

What then are the low-level intervention strategies you need to master? This chapter explores a range of these subtle teaching techniques. For ease of explanation, they have been grouped under three subheadings: nudging, refocusing and reminding. Generally speaking, they are ordered from least through to most intrusive intervention. This does not mean they have to be used in sequence. Classroom management is about finding the right strategy for the situation, not a slavish adherence to a nominated sequence of steps. ('Michaela, you set my desk on fire – that is your first warning.') Rather your guiding principle here should be finding the lowest level intervention that works in that situation (Pearsall, 2020). Could you use any of these strategies more than you currently do?

> Your guiding principle here should be finding the lowest level intervention that works in that situation.

Nudging

Nudges are the small adjustments of practice that correct a student's behaviour without them even being aware of what you are doing. I like how a participant in a video coaching session once defined nudges to me: 'It's about being good at all those things you do that that seem like you are not doing anything at all.' Precisely.

TACTICAL IGNORING OF THE STUDENT

Sometimes the best strategy when dealing with off-task behaviour is to do nothing. If a student is exhibiting low-level attention seeking, usually the most effective technique is to simply ignore them. Of course, if the student is distracting others, you may not be able to use this technique. However, if you assess that their behaviour is not substantially interrupting the rest of the class, it is worth trying this approach. Often just showing an attention-seeking student that you will not be distracted by their behaviour is enough to nudge them back to their work.

ON-TASK PRAISE

In classroom management it is not what you say 'no' to but what you say 'yes' to that often matters most. When a student is distracted or slow to start their work, the impulse of many teachers is to immediately address this behaviour directly with the student. This is not always the lowest level intervention you could use. Indeed, you may be able to change their behaviour without having to interact with them at all. Using on-task praise – acknowledging students who are doing the right thing – is often enough to remind those who are off task to get back to what they were meant to be doing. The nuances of how you do this matter a great deal. Keep the following ideas in mind when using on-task praise.

> It is not what you say 'no' to but what you say 'yes' to that often matters most.

Be authentic

Students are quick to see through empty praise ('Great posture!') when it is directed at them let alone when directed at classmates. Avoid saccharine compliments and generic affirmations. Watch carefully what students are doing in class and be quick to affirm those students who are on track in concrete and specific terms:

> *Greg is underway, already started question two.*
>
> *Marley has got straight to it, rewriting the contention.*

This helps create a 'bread crumb trail' of suggestions as to what is required of the student who is off task and lets them hear about their classmates' progress on the set task.

Praise effort over ability

If we want to encourage our students to have a growth mindset, we don't praise who they are but what they do (Dweck, 2017). This is perhaps even more important when we are using on-task praise to shape a student's behaviour. Remember it is the off-task student's *effort* that we are trying to engage or cue into action. It is easy for many students to ignore praise that is aimed at another student if it is about their character. Since it doesn't seem to have anything to do with them personally ('Great, Milla, you're a star!').

Low-key interventions

Whereas concentrating on behaviours rather than the person praise is directed to ('Karen as tried that three times before she got it right – that's the persistence we are trying to use.') is something they are much more likely to emulate.

Not only is on-task praise subtly effective on individual students but it also helps create a positive classroom culture for the entire group. This is because 'describing what most people do in a particular situation encourages others to do the same' (Service et al., 2014, p. 5). By affirming the practice you want to see more of, you increase the likelihood that students will mirror this behaviour and help 'crowd out' behaviours that are problematic.

Of course, catching your students working well is not always easy. I have chosen the word catching here because sometimes it takes real energy and vigilance to spot the students doing the right thing. (In fact, acknowledging that students who routinely don't do the right thing but are working well is, in my experience, often a particularly powerful motivator. Keep an eye out for opportunities to do this.) This effort is worth it, though, because it means you approach teaching with a positive mindset. You go into class looking to acknowledge students who are doing the right thing, looking to celebrate the best version of how students might approach their learning.

PROXIMITY WITHOUT EYE CONTACT

It is a common tactic for teachers to stand near a student to encourage them to get back to their work. However, for this to be an effective nudge, you need to do this while withholding eye contact. Walking up to a student or group of students who are not on task and looking directly at them will usually succeed in getting them back to their learning. However, we need to remember our goal here is a more subtle intervention where the student doesn't realise they are being influenced. We want to avoid habituating our classes into always needing this kind of cueing. We want to avoid the situation where for some students 'I get back to work when you give me attention' can become 'I will only get back to work when you give me attention.'

There are a couple of things to keep in mind when using proximity.

Be aware of spacing

Positioning is crucial here. You need to stand close enough to the student to catch their attention without being so close that you are in their personal space or that they feel your proximity is targeting them. Standing beside the student a metre or so away, or at a forty-five-degree angle if you must be in front of them, seems to work best. Do not stand directly behind the student as this can make them feel uncomfortable.

Note their reaction

Using your peripheral vision, take careful note of how the student responds to your proximity. If they look to you or back to their work, that is a clear sign they are responding to your presence. Sometimes these signs are subtle (a slight shift in posture or quick glance at their laptop), but even a minor change is a good predictor that the student has noticed you and may reorientate themselves back to their learning.

Be ready to refine

Of course, this doesn't happen every time or even the majority of the time. Rather than abandoning the strategy if it doesn't work, make some quick adjustments and see if that has the desired effect. If you are standing somewhere in front of the student and it didn't work, try moving more directly into their line of sight. If you are standing beside them shift back at a forty-five-degree angle to the edge of their peripheral vision and see if that cues their attention. One of the most effective adjustments is to try using proximity again, but this time address the whole class as you do it. I find that speaking to the group – offering some general praise or adding an instruction about the work – is an easy way to reiterate my proximity without seeming as though I am directly targeting a student.

Using this proximity as a strategy has the welcome benefit of reminding you of the power of your presence in the classroom. Making sure you are constantly moving around the room, interacting with every student, makes for dynamic and engaged teaching but also creates opportunities to nudge students back on task in a quick, low-key way.

CROSS PRAISE

Cross praise, which is also known as *parallel cueing*, is a combination of on-task praise and proximity. To cross praise a student you identify another student who is working well and then position yourself so that when you acknowledge their efforts, the praise is delivered across the off-task student, cueing that student to get back to work. Cross praise is a subtle technique, but is easy to learn and implement if you are mindful of two things: positioning and the student's reaction.

Positioning

Be mindful about where you and each of the students involved are situated in the room. Cross praise is often modelled to trainee teachers as the technique where you compliment the student sitting next to the one who is off task. You don't always need to target your off-task student's immediate neighbour though. How often, after all, is it that the student who is off task has someone working studiously right beside them? You just need to ensure that the praise you deliver 'passes across the off-task student, including them within your conversation' (Pearsall, 2020 p. 17). Cross praise can work when the off-task student is in the front row and the student who is being praised is in the back row. Indeed, I often see cross praise used effectively by experienced teachers right across large open learning spaces or all the way down the other end of a gymnasium. If your praise passes by the student you are targeting, even in large or outdoor spaces, you have a good chance of catching their attention.

Watch the student's reaction

Take careful note of how the student responds to cross praise. It is a subtle technique, and sometimes teachers underestimate its effectiveness. This is less likely to happen if you teach very young kids who tend to respond to cross praise in an obvious way. ('I'm sitting up straight too!') If you are watching carefully, though, you will see that older students respond just as immediately – just not as overtly. Watch to see if they turn their head or body slightly in your direction or towards the student you are praising. Be on the lookout for a change in their eyeline – a glance up from what they were doing or down to their work. These minor movements are often a good indication that they have heard you and may get back to the learning.

I really like using cross praise because it draws on students' awareness of their peers. Many classroom management strategies rest on the idea that students will change their behaviour because they respect their teacher's authority or strong relationship with them. However, many students are much more responsive to their classmates. ('They are way more loyal to each other than to me,' an experienced teacher who taught me this technique once told me. 'So why not use that?') Cross praise gives you a way to use this connectedness to shape the communal behaviour of the group.

Don't expect these techniques to work instantaneously. After using each of these nudges I like to give my students some time before I see if they have worked. Typically, after using a nudge I move to another part of the room to give the student a chance to resettle and from there, I can monitor unobtrusively whether this strategy was effective or whether I need to use a more overt intervention.

Refocusing

Refocusing strategies represent your next level of intervention. While usually subtle, they nonetheless represent an escalation of response because students know you are guiding them to get back to their learning. Here are some examples of refocusing that, if used with care, can encourage students to get back to their work.

CHECK INS

You can encourage a student to get back to what they were doing with a word of encouragement or quick chat about their progress.

Collective progress check

Probably the simplest way to touch base with students in this way is a collective check in, where you aim your inquiries towards a group that includes the student whose off-task behaviour you are trying to address.

At first, you might do this non-verbally. Approach the group of students and make a show of scanning their work. Make sure your demeanour is friendly – you want to seem curious not disapproving. Try to peruse every student's efforts, but don't dwell on any one response.

Some teachers like to begin a group check in by announcing that they are now going to check on everyone's progress. Often just the announcement is enough to change the student's behaviour before you even get to scanning their work. This works particularly well if you have previously reviewed your students' work because they know that you have a benchmark against which to measure their progress. For example, if your students are working on paper, you can sign each student's work at the point they are up to in their workbooks and check their progress ten or fifteen minutes later to see how much they have done in that time.

If a non-verbal check doesn't work or suit the context, do this as a verbal inquiry. Again, the key here is addressing a group of students rather than an individual:

How are we going here?

Is everyone able to get started?

Does anyone have questions about the work?

This is often enough to remind the student what you expect everyone to be doing.

Occasionally, the student you are targeting will see this as an opportunity for some attention-seeking behaviour. Anticipate that some students will respond this way. Bold assertions of success on behalf of the group ('We are all over this, Mr Pearsall!') often accompanied by duper's delight – the subtle smile that people display when telling a pleasing lie – are not uncommon. You can deal with this by just refocusing your attention on the individual. ('Great Stephen, let me have look what you are working on.')

Individual progress check

When checking on individual students, you ask similar questions but just targeted directly at the student themselves.

How is it going?

What are you working on?

Do you think you can meet all the success criteria?

The big difference is that you have to pay extra attention to *how* the question is delivered. You don't want the student to act defensive, so signal to them that you are offering assistance not judgement. Make sure you adopt a warm expression and friendly tone. Concentrate on using open body language and relaxed gestures. ('What are you working on?' is a very different question when delivered with crossed arms and a sharp tone.)

Encouragement

Another way to check in on an off-task student is to offer them some brief words of encouragement:

You can do it. This exercise gets easier with practice.

You've shown good persistence. Keep going.

Five minutes to go. You are nearly done.

Encouragement in this context is a form of on-task praise that focuses on persistence. You want to reassure the off-task student that with effort they have the capacity to do what is being asked of them. This, of course, isn't always effective (I once had a student respond: 'I know I can do it; it's just that I don't want to!'), but encouragement does often work well as a check in – particularly if the student's behaviour is generated by low confidence or if they are feeling a lack of support or attention. A little targeted praise here can go a long way.

NON-VERBAL COMMANDS

Most teachers already use wordless glances or gestures to direct students back to what they are meant to be doing. The appeal of these strategies is that you don't have to interrupt what you are teaching to employ them. You might be working one-on-one with a student, listening to them read a response while at the same time looking on silently at a group that is distracted. The student who you are working with isn't interrupted by this, but the unruly group gets a clear reminder of your expectations. A raised eyebrow, pausing and looking towards an off-task student, pointing to what a student should be doing or raising an open palm to indicate they need to halt what they are doing are popular examples of non-verbal reminders. What follows are some things to keep in mind when using them.

Be precise
Using unambiguous expressions and clear, direct gestures is at the heart of effective non-verbal communication. When coaching, I often find myself using the adjective *crisp* to describe the manner of teachers who are good non-verbal communicators. They are decisive in their movements, conveying what they want the students to do in a precise manner. Body language experts describe those with this kind of precise manner as having *great phrasing* (Bradley, 2019; Gladwell, 2009). These teachers deliver non-verbal instructions as short, sharp signals and then pivot immediately back to their teaching. When you do this, it gives the sense that you are used to students complying with your instruction and is a good way to 'fake it till you make it.'

Use micro signals
Once students are responding to your non-verbal reminders, make them *smaller*: blocking a behaviour with palm held at arms-length might become a raised index finger close to the body. Shaking your head with a stern expression might become a raised eyebrow. Making your movements more economical encourages students to watch you more closely and, over time, allows you to shape student behaviour with fewer interruptions from them or extra effort from you.

Table tapping

Table tapping is a good example of a simple non-verbal strategy that is more effective if you keep these pieces of advice in mind.

Approach the off-task student from side-on and tap on their desk as a cue for them to get back to work. Make your movements deliberate: remain side-on to the student withholding eye contact, bend from the waist and, making sure your hand is well away from their work, tap twice. If this doesn't refocus their attention, you might try tapping slightly closer to them or even adjusting their work by turning the corner of their workbook or device to get a better view of their work. Once students are used to this cue, you can make it smaller by just briefly resting a finger on the table as you pass by the students.

This might seem a minor adjustment of practice, but it is precisely this sort of subtle use of technique that is the hallmark of highly effective teachers.

Reminding

If nudging and refocusing aren't effective or appropriate for altering a student's behaviour, you might try a reminder. These are strategies that you use to reiterate your expectations to students and to remind them of their commitment to 'agreed class behaviours'.

CLASS REMINDERS

At first, reminders are usually addressed to the wider class rather than a specific student. Lemov (2015), for example, calls this type of reminder a *positive group correction* to distinguish it from a *private individual correction*. Of course, teachers issue general reminders to their classes all the time. ('Quiet please.' 'Eyes this way.') This is not what I am referring to here. In this technique, the idea is that by reminding the whole class about your expectations you can, in a non-confrontational way, encourage individual students to get back to the task. It is for this reason that Lewis (2008) labels this type of intervention a *hint*.

Isn't this the same as on-task praise? On-task praise *is* similar to class reminders. There are some differences, though. With on-task praise you deliver a running commentary – what Lemov (2015, p. 431) calls 'narration' – that acknowledges individual students who are meeting that lesson's goals:

> *I can see Sam has started. Grayson and Kyle are underway.*

Whereas class reminders address the whole class and comment on communal and personal responsibilities – with the clear implication that some students are not meeting these goals.

> *Nearly everyone has started responsibly by immediately getting underway.*

These reminders might talk about the gap between behaviour and expectation in a general way or by specifically naming an aspect of student practice. Here are two representative examples of a general hint offered by Lewis (2008, p. 46):

> *Just about everyone appears to be respecting their classmates' rights.*
>
> *Some students aren't encouraging their friends to behave responsibly.*

Or you might talk about student behaviour in less generic terms:

> *I can see a number of students following our spiderweb conversation protocol.*
>
> *Not all students are handling the archery equipment in the way we talked about in our safety briefing.*

Note that one of these examples frames the behaviour positively and the other negatively, but they both follow a similar structure. The teacher describes what they are seeing but doesn't present any specific demand about what they want the students to do. The required action is implied. You make the class aware that a problem exists and trust the individual students involved to self-regulate their behaviour.

Ramon Lewis (2008) also recommends a third variation of reminder, one in which you reiterate 'the understanding shared within the class about what is responsible behaviour' (p. 48). The best way to do this is to remind students explicitly that these are *shared* norms:

> *We agreed that we wouldn't talk over each other.*
>
> *We said that we would all speak respectfully.*

A good deal of the decisions we make are heavily influenced by what those around us do (Pentland, 2014). Referring to collective expectations about behaviour adds weight to this style of reminder – this is not just your expectation but their peers' too – and I have found it particularly effective guiding students back to their work. (For further discussion of this see 'Rights and responsibility reminders' in Chapter 2.)

ANONYMOUS INDIVIDUAL REMINDERS

If a class reminder doesn't work, you could switch to issuing a directive (see Chapter 2), but targeting the students involved with some anonymous feedback is worth a try first. You do this by alluding to specific students without naming them, implying that they need to change their behaviour in some way:

> *I am still waiting on one student.*
>
> *I can see that all but two of you have followed the instruction.*
>
> *I am waiting for one group to put their equipment down safely.*

This isn't very different from just naming the student and giving them a directive, but its anonymous nature tends to elicit less resistance – especially from those students who feel like you are singling them out because you have to name them constantly to get them back on task.

OBSERVATION PROMPT

If issuing reminders to the whole class hasn't succeeded, I will often try to remind off-task students of my expectations by quietly noting evidence to them that their actions don't meet my expectations. To initiate an observation prompt, approach the student and flag some aspect of their behaviour:

> *I noticed you closed your book.*
>
> *I can see you didn't put your phone away yet.*
>
> *I noticed you were not at your desk.*

This approach should allow you to start a conversation in a non-combative way about what the student needs to start doing. Observation prompts take a bit of practice to master, as there are some potential traps to avoid. If you are trialling this technique you need to be conscious of a couple of things, which are explored here.

Keep it warm

As with progress checks, you need to ensure that your tone is warm and body language relaxed. The prompt should be a friendly inquiry not a pointed accusation, and students will decide which of these it is based as much on how you say it as what you say.

Be descriptive

You do not want to come off as being judgemental. Simply describe what you are seeing without including any sense of how you feel about this behaviour. The technical term for feedback that withholds emotional judgement is *non-attributive* (Kegan & Lahey, 2002). The observation prompts described earlier are non-attributive. Here's how they might sound if they were attributive:

> *I noticed you couldn't be bothered persisting and closed your book.*
>
> *I can see you still haven't put your phone away.*
>
> *I noticed you were wandering around the class aimlessly.*

By withholding emotional judgment, you make it more likely that students will not become defensive when you point out their off-task behaviour and thus more likely that they will be open to altering what they are doing.

Given that in an open prompt you directly address the student and point out aspects of their off-task behaviour, it is possible to argue that they are not reminders at all. (I did, for example, contemplate putting open prompts in the next chapter on directives.) However, because in the end you are not telling the student what to do but merely flagging evidence of what they are currently doing, they are more accurately characterised as a subtle form of reminder. This subtlety – they are sometimes known as *non-directives* or *invisible commands* – is the strength of this technique and why they are worth giving a shot before you move to explicitly telling students what they need to do to change their behaviour.

Conclusion

In coaching sessions, I frequently play video excerpts of accomplished teachers nudging, refocusing and reminding students of what they need to be doing to stay on task. Participants often remark at the range of techniques that expert teachers have to draw on. ('I wouldn't have thought to do that; I would've just started yelling.') The key to dealing with low-level off-task behaviour is having this wide array of options from which to choose. Having multiple ways to address these behaviours means you can use this approach repeatedly without having to escalate your intervention so you can concentrate your energies what matters most – student learning.

Chapter 2
Giving explicit instructions

I once received a call from a tertiary teaching institution inviting me to deliver a keynote on building positive classroom behaviours: 'We hear you have lots of practical strategies for helping young people avoid their worst behaviours.'

I could barely make out this offer because my sons, six and eight, were standing a metre from me both emitting a series of strange groans. 'Guys, could you please cut out the zombie noises?' I asked.

Instead of altering their behaviour, my request sent them into paroxysms of laughter and shouting ('Zombies!'), and then they stomped around the room in a stiff-legged, undead shuffle – groaning even more loudly than before.

'Well, I have strategies for helping *some* young people avoid their worst behaviours.'

Offering instructions and giving commands in a classroom takes real expertise. You have to find the right type of command for the context – and deliver it with precise phrasing and a nuanced awareness of tone and body language. Sometimes even a single word is enough to undermine your message. (My exchange with my boys would have been more effective if I hadn't mentioned zombies but simply said, 'Could you please cut out the noises?')

Given that this is hard to do during a hectic lesson, I think it is useful to have a range of *intervention scripts* to help you work out how to respond to this off-task behaviour. These scripts are not a word-for-word account of what to say in each situation but rather a scaffold that you can use to quickly formulate a response. In this chapter, you will find a selection of these scripts for offering commands and giving directives to students. Could any of these approaches be added to your repertoire?

Simple instruction

A simple instruction is where you give a student a straightforward direction. There are lots of different ways to approach issuing instruction, but there are some guiding principles to keep in mind: be affirming, be brief and be patient.

BE AFFIRMING

Try to name the behaviour you want not the behaviour you don't want. Of course, there are lots of times when you have to focus on what students are doing wrong. Where possible though, describe precisely what you expect the student to do to comply with your instruction:

> *Josh, open your book and start at problem two, thank you.*
>
> *Linda, please begin your turn and talk now.*

I like this approach because you are less likely to use attributive language – you are describing a solution not what the student did wrong. Moreover, you don't have to debate with the student whether the problem occurred at all. This makes for both clearer instruction and a more positive classroom environment.

BE BRIEF

Simple instruction needs to be concise. Rather than let yourself become entangled in explanations or justification, state clearly what the student needs to do differently and pivot straight back to your teaching:

> *Kim, sit up straight, thank you.*
>
> *Safety goggles on, thanks Chris.*

> Be concise. Rather than let yourself become entangled in explanations or justification, state clearly what the student needs to do differently and pivot straight back to your teaching.

The key to doing this well is not just having a clear and concise instruction in mind but also an exit point. Before you give a simple instruction, think about how to close the conversation. Note in the examples that each instruction finishes with a definitive end point ('now' and 'thank you') that concludes the exchange. This is about not only how you word your instruction but also how you use your body language. Once you issue an instruction, move or turn away from the student to indicate the matter is concluded and you presume that they are about to comply with your request.

BE PATIENT

Obviously, students don't always comply, but don't rush to reiterate your instruction. Give students take-up time to process your request and get themselves back to their learning. There are all sorts of reasons why students might not comply immediately. They might just need a moment to get their heads around what it is that they have to do next – a delay associated with cognitive switching is natural (Horvath, 2019) – or want to signal to their peers that they aren't cowed by your authority. Anticipating that there might be a delay between your instruction and their response means you repeat yourself less (and appear more authoritative), and your students are given a realistic time frame in which to change their behaviour.

> Give students take-up time to process your request and get themselves back to their learning.

INVERTED INSTRUCTION

This is one of my favourite variations on a simple instruction. Instead of asking a student to do something and then thanking them:

Erin, put your rubbish in the bin, thank you.

You invert the command so that you are thanking them for something they are about to do:

Thank you for putting your rubbish in the bin Erin.

Sometimes known as a respectful command, I like that this approach is both firm and polite. Framing the instruction as a 'thank you' implies compliance and allows you to demand a change of student behaviour in a non-confrontational way.

As this example suggests, there are lots of subtle variations you can make to the simple instructions you use to address student behaviour. Whatever variation you employ, keep in mind the principles outlined when you trial what works best in your classroom.

MICRO COMMANDS

Let's look a little deeper at one of the principles of simple instruction: being brief.

Brevity of instruction is the hallmark of authority in many fields of endeavour. Leaders of organisations, for example, write shorter emails than those of their subordinates (Pennebaker, 2013). We see this pattern in the classrooms of accomplished teachers, who tend to use very brief injections to get students back on track. We label these brief interjections *micro commands*.

A micro command is a short, sharp reiteration of your expectations. For this reason, it is best to have a small bank of micro commands that you use repeatedly. Your students quickly learn what these commands mean and can follow them without you having to offer further explanation. Here are some versatile micro commands you might use in your classes.

'Inappropriate time'

You can use this micro command to skirt around having to unpack irrelevant issues or deal with off-task interruptions.

For example, in primary school settings, the time immediately after lunch can be taxing on teachers as their students arrive back to class wanting their teacher to resolve incidents that have occurred in the yard: 'Eden took the bat tennis bats, but we booked them just on the wrong day, and now Coen and Piers say we are lying!'

Rather than become immersed in this issue, wave the students off with an 'inappropriate time'. (I like to shake my head and point to the learning goal for that lesson as I do this.) As long as you follow up later, students will quickly learn when and how to ask for your attention. For example, in this specific instance, that there is a dedicated time or process for dispute resolution.

In high school settings you sometimes encounter students who are highly skilled – and much practised – at distracting teachers from their lesson plan.

When one of these students tries to sidetrack you with a personal question, irrelevant request ('Can we play dead fish?') or long digression, pull them up short with an 'inappropriate time' and pivot straight back to the learning.

'Not negotiable'

You can use this micro command to address begging and bargaining. Many students will demonstrate resistance not by outright refusal but by treating their compliance as conditional:

> *I'll get started if you just let me finish my game.*
> *Can I go back to my locker and then I'll do it?*

Similarly, students will sometimes pester teachers with repeated requests for alternative tasks or to be excused from having to complete their set work:

> *Can't I just skip this? It is so boring!*

'Not negotiable' is a micro command that lets you quickly address these requests without having to go into elaborate justification of why students need to do what is asked of them.

'Not here' and 'not now'

You can use these commands to remind students that their behaviour needs to be appropriate for the classroom context.

I like using 'not here', for example, because it is proportional and respectful. You are not saying what the student is doing is inherently wrong; it is just not suitable for the classroom. You employ 'not now' in a similar way, using it to signal that what the student is doing is not appropriate at this point in the lesson. (You might also try 'later, thanks' or 'wait, thank you' to do this.)

Both 'not here' and 'not now' are gentler than an emphatic 'no' or 'don't' but generate similar results. It is for this reason that they are a popular command among experienced classroom teachers.

'No put-downs'

This is a quick catchall term you can use to address all kinds of verbal bullying or inappropriate talk.

Every classroom should have a 'no put-down' rule. You need to make clear to every student that they are not allowed to say anything to a classmate (or you for that matter) that is scornful or pejorative in any way. 'No put-downs' is a shorthand reminder of all of the expectations you have developed around avoiding bullying behaviour. You can use it quickly to cut off a student who is starting to say something inappropriate to a classmate or remind another that while they might just be joking, the target of their comment might not take it that way. 'No put-downs' is probably the most impactful of all micro commands and an essential one to have in your repertoire.

Of course, this is far from an exhaustive list of micro commands. You will have your own favourites. (I know that for some teachers 'away, thanks' has become essential in the smartphone era.) The examples I have listed here should stand as a clear example of the kind of succinct phrases we can use to check our students off-task behaviour.

Rights and responsibilities reminders

I find that it is often easier to address off-task behaviour by citing the student's rights and responsibilities than it is to cite your personal authority. This makes sense. 'Do it because I told you to' is not as powerful as 'Do it because it is our rule' – particularly if these rights and responsibilities have been developed with stakeholder input from the student and their peers.

> It is often easier to address off-task behaviour by citing the student's rights and responsibilities than it is to cite your personal authority.

RULE PROMPTS

Rule prompts, which are sometimes also called agreement prompts, are the simplest form of this kind of reminder. When one of your students is doing something that they shouldn't be doing, you point out to them the agreed expectation and describe how they can change their behaviour to meet this expectation:

> *Matt, remember our rule about wearing our safety equipment at all times? Put your safety goggles, thank you.*

This straightforward intervention is not that different from a simple instruction. Adding the opening line though helps depersonalise the encounter – you are simply reminding them of an already established rule.

Moreover, the line reiterates that this is a whole-class responsibility you are citing. (Note the careful use of 'our', for example.)

Citing past efforts

One variation of a rule prompt is to not remind the student explicitly of the rule but previous times when they met this expectation. Paul Dix (2017) popularised a version of this approach as a *thirty-second script*. It has four parts:

1. You open with an 'I noticed' statement pointing out that the student isn't yet on task.

    I noticed you have not ... got underway yet/joined your group yet/ attempted all the questions.

2. Then cite a time when a student was working well in a similar situation.

    Do you remember last lesson when you ... were so quick to start/ contributed really well to your group/showed such great persistence?

3. Ask students to emulate this behaviour.

    That's the attitude/approach/behaviour/student I want to see today ...

4. Close the encounter by thanking the student for their time and quickly moving on to give them some take-up time.

    Thanks for listening.

This thirty-second intervention is incredibly versatile. You should find that, with practice, you can use it in in lots of different classroom situations to remind students of the best version of their own behaviour.

IDID

The IDID protocol is a more sophisticated version of a rule prompt reminder. It was developed by Ramon Lewis (2008) and is designed to prompt students to consider the impact of their behaviour. (Lewis doesn't call it IDID, but I find it easier to remember it that way – it is the strategy you use to prompt a student to ask themselves the impact of 'what I did'.) It has four simple steps:

1. **I**dentify the student.

    Amil,

2. **D**escribe the behaviour.

    You are shouting.

3. **I**dentify the right being denied.

   Everyone has the right to work without distraction.

4. **D**emand responsible behaviour.

   Classroom voice, thank you.

Again, the nuances of how this intervention script is phrased and delivered matter here. When you identify the student, make sure your voice is loud enough to get their attention, but the moment you have it, drop your voice to a conversational register to describe their behaviour. Use non-attributive terms to describe what they are doing. Students are less likely to interrupt you here if you are talking in a calm voice and using unemotive language to depict their behaviour.

You also need to make sure you close the encounter with a clear instruction about how they can get back on task. The last *D* in IDID is sometimes characterised as *describe*, but I think *demand* is better because it reminds us that we are not giving the student an option – we are insisting that they don't infringe on the rights of others.

This focus on the rights of others (the third line of the script) is the most important part to get right with this style of intervention. It is also the most challenging. You want to make sure that you explicitly tie the student's off-task behaviour to the infringement of specific rights of the other class members. This helps students see the 'assumptions underlying (your) intervention' (Lewis, 2008, p. 63). You are not singling them out or picking on them for personal reasons but rather reminding them of their commitment to their peers. Here are some examples of how you might phrase this third line:

Every student has the right to feel safe in class.

I have the right to speak without interruption.

She has the right to be heard without having to worry about put-downs.

Coming late means I have to start again. This is not fair to those who were on time.

Playing games on your computer distracts others too.

When you first put this technique into action, use the word *rights* to make the connection between the student's actions and the right being denied as evident as possible. (Note how this is done in the first three examples.) Once it is a more established practice you don't have to be as descriptive.

(The last two examples here don't mention rights but clearly still refer to them.)

The IDID technique takes a while to feel natural, but is worth practising as it is a highly effective way to remind the class to be mindful of each other's rights.

Acknowledging scripts

Teacher interventions don't happen in a vacuum. There is always an emotional context to the events that led up to the off-task behaviour and your immediate response to it. Sometimes we need to acknowledge that context (see the acknowledgement prompts in Chapter 4). The two strategies in this section give you a way to do this. The ECA intervention offers you a script for acknowledging your student's feelings about the situation that might have led to the off-task behaviour. The *I statement* technique allows you to calmly convey to them the emotional impact of their behaviour on you. Recognising the emotions that are shaping the context of the incident gives you a way to acknowledge the legitimacy of these feelings and then pivot back to practical steps needed to address the behaviour.

ECA

I once observed a teacher on a forty-two-degree day censuring a student for not listening properly and slumping at their desk. The student was outraged. ('But it is so hot.') This was an understandable response – there was no air conditioning, and the room felt like a kiln. To the outrage of his classmates, the teacher tried to push past this response. ('Look, it is not that hot and …') Before she could finish a cacophony of protests and complaints erupted, derailing the lesson. Acknowledging that the students were in a trying situation ('I know that is hot in here and difficult to concentrate …') before offering a reminder about behaviour might have helped avoid this happening.

The ECA is a technique you can use to make sure you avoid this trap. ECA stands for *empathy, content, action*.

- **E:** Start your intervention by *empathising* with the student's mood.
  This is not merely sympathising – you are not just showing concern but demonstrating that you can see the situation from their perspective.

> *I know this work is challenging, Phuong, and we have been doing it for a long time.*

- **C:** Then you make a *content* statement that describes what is taking place in the class that needs to change. Avoid using emotive terms or passing judgement on what you are seeing. (Sometimes people call this intervention EDA to emphasise that the content statement is a concrete *description* not a critical comment.) Simply describe what you are seeing that is concerning you.

  However, I can see that some of you are off task, and it is distracting the rest of us.

- **A:** Finally, state the *action* you want the students to take to remedy the situation.

  If you are finished or need a change of pace, could you please start your traffic light summary? That way we all can be on task.

The key thing to work on in this script is the *E*. When I train teachers in this technique, they quickly become accomplished at describing what students are doing wrong or insisting on how to remedy this situation but need practice at acknowledging the context that is driving that behaviour. Get this phase right, though, and this script can be unusually effective. Jenny Mackay (2020), who invented this technique, suggests that 'tuning in' to your students in this way helps 'you make a connection that invites cooperation' (p. 44). This is certainly my experience of the ECA technique. Try this script in your class and see if it has a similar effect.

I STATEMENTS

It is not just our students' feelings we need to acknowledge. Sometimes we need to acknowledge our own emotions too. This can seem counterintuitive. Generally, classroom management techniques require us to separate our emotional reactions from our personal responses, and it is, therefore, understandable that teachers might think there is no room for their own emotions to be part of the response to off-task behaviour.

This isn't really being fair to ourselves. We are stakeholders in the class too. We can't be expected to simply endure poor behaviour without acknowledging the effect that it may have on us. It is important, after all, that students understand that their behaviour impacts on those around them – including their teacher.

I statements allow you to speak to student behaviour in a manner that acknowledges your personal response but frames that response in a professional way (Rogers et al., 2018). As the name suggests, an I statement focuses not on what the student did ('You threw that …') but the effect that it had on you ('I get scared when …').

We can break I statements – some theorists prefer *I messages* – into three constituent parts:

1. Describe the behaviour.

   When you ignore my instructions,
2. State your feelings.

   I feel disrespected.
3. Describe the (potential) consequences of the student's actions.

   These kinds of interruptions make it hard for me to assist your classmates or for you to get my help.

That students should, therefore, change their behaviour is implicit in this instruction. However, Mackay (2020) has suggested that you do this explicitly by reiterating what the student should do to change the situation as a final step:

So, I expect you to follow my instruction and get back to the task.

I prefer to do it this way at first and then, as students become more tuned in to my I statements, skip this last step.

Whether you include this step or not, I statements can be really effective. You just need to be careful about how you state your feelings. This is more than just starting with an *I*. ('I really hate how you wrecked this for everyone' is not an I message.) Be mindful of body language and make sure your tone is not accusatory. Avoid the language of blame. You want to model to the student that you can be upset or angry without having to act that way.

I statements are ideal for dealing with 'very strong emotions' as they 'allow you to take responsibility for your own feelings' while also addressing student behaviour (Mackay, 2006, p. 56). If you find yourself routinely getting caught in a cycle of accusation and defiance with a student whenever you intervene with their behaviour, this script might be a more appropriate response.

Conclusion

Looking back over the intervention scripts explored in this chapter, it can seem that there is not a huge difference between each technique we have explored. For example, 'Safety goggles on, thanks Chris' and 'Matt, remember our rule about wearing our safety equipment at all times? Put your safety goggles back on, thank you' might sound like they are effectively the same exchange.

However, I think this is the point. The difference between a successful intervention where one of your students gets back to their work and one where your instruction is ignored – or even leads to conflict – is often very subtle. Little changes of wording and approach matter a great deal. Sometimes when our attempts to alter a student's behaviour don't work, our impulse is not to look at these minor adjustments but to go bigger, to be louder or more emphatic. More often the solution though is not an increase in volume and vehemence but a small shift in your practice.

This chapter offers you an array of these small shifts to trial in your classroom. At first the scripts offered here might seem awkward or stilted, but with a little practice and modification they will come to feel like a natural, almost automatic, part of your everyday teaching.

Of course, just because you deliver these techniques well doesn't mean that students won't resist or argue back. In the next two chapters we explore what we do when these strategies don't work.

Chapter 3
Low-demand instruction

There are some students though where the issue is not *how you give instructions* but that *you are giving instructions at all*.

When I work with a school, there are usually at least one or two students who demonstrate this kind of demand-avoidant response to instruction. These are students who outright refuse to complete their work, get into protracted arguments about following simple requests and even baulk at taking part in activities that they will seemingly enjoy.

Supporting these students is tricky. Recently, I watched a highly-skilled teacher deal with a resistant student by offering her a directed choice: 'do you want to work with a group or over on the craft table?' The students made a quick decision and was on her way to her group when the teacher thanked her. Abruptly, she stopped. The 'thank you' recast her actions not as her decision but as something she was doing *for* the teacher. Instead of walking over to classmates she changed direction and headed to the white board. There, glaring at the teacher the whole time, she methodically wiped off all of the instruction the teacher had placed on the board for that lesson.

Students who exhibit demand-avoidant behaviour, read teacher demands as attempts to take control of them. They need a high degree of autonomy to feel comfortable in class and often have a raised threat response when they feel their independence is being compromised.

When viewed through this lens, many inexplicable acts of 'defiance' and sudden classroom 'tantrums' actually seem like a logical response to a heightened feeling of threat.

I once asked a student what it felt like when he was told to do something by a teacher. He was a Year 12 student who'd recently started driving lessons and he responded with a neat analogy: it was like you were driving a car and someone suddenly grabbed the wheel and started steering. 'Do you feel that way', I asked him, 'even if what the teacher is asking you is something you actually want to do?' He responded by asking me if I was driving somewhere I wanted to go, would I like it if my passenger grabbed the wheel?

Given that there are dozens of moments in every lesson where you might have to provide instruction that could feel like a threatening demand, how do you help these students?

One suggested response is that you have to create a *low-demand environment* for that student. Reduce the total number of demands you place on the student, give them lots of choice, helping to build their feelings of safety and autonomy in the classroom. Indeed, one of the pieces advice I hear most often from coordinators who are trying to support a colleague with demand-avoidant student is 'pick your battles'.

Creating a low-demand environment is an effective strategy for supporting these students. However, even if a teacher does this effectively, the so-called 'battles' can be explosive. You may have built a high degree of autonomy into the students individual learning plan, used routine to subtly encourage the student to focus on their learning, employed non-verbals to nudge them back on task when they are being distracted and tactically-ignored behaviour that in another student you would have immediately addressed – but sooner or later you have to tell the student to do something (or stop doing something) and this leads to conflict.

The best way I have found to reduce the frequency and intensity of these 'blow ups' is to change how you give instruction to demand-avoidant students.

Declarative language

Teaching is full of moments when we have to *get* our students to do things. Typically this is done with imperatives:

>   *OK, answer Question Two and then do the graph.*

>   *Sit down, thanks.*

>   *Form into groups of three please.*

>   *Start your work.*

An imperative is any statement that demands a specific action. When I do video analysis of classes there are scores of imperatives in every lesson.

However, it is just these kinds of statements that can trigger a flight, fight or freeze response from demand-avoidant students (Cat, 2018).

We can shift this dynamic by replacing imperatives with declarative language. Declarative language doesn't demand action, but rather subtly suggests it:

I notice that it is 3pm.

The Principal is about to speak.

Rather than telling your students what to do, these statements provide the information that will cue their action. They encourage students to become more aware of what is required of them and, over time, teach them to show more in agency in their own learning.

When approaching a situation with a resistant or reluctant student, you are not thinking what you need to *get* them to do so much as what can you *give* them to make it easier to show their own initiative. Here are five examples of imperative statements that have been reframed as declaratives:

Line up now please.
I can see the others lining up.

Everyone turn to page 47
Page 47 is the start of the chapter.

Put your bag on the hook.
Your bag is on the floor.

Serve the ball!
Your friend is awaiting serve.

Pack up.
The bell is going.

Rather than *ordering* students to do something these declarative statements *invite* students to consider their response. This maintains their sense of autonomy but makes it more likely that they will take action.

> Many inexplicable acts of 'defiance' and sudden classroom 'tantrums' are actually responses to a heightened feeling of threat.

Constructing declarative statements

In my experience, employing declarative statements can be highly effective but it takes time to hone this technique. Teachers don't usually give classroom instructions in the declarative form so you will need to put some thought into how you construct these statements. Here's a list of suggestions based on *The Declarative Language Handbook* (Murphy, 2020) of how to do this.

INVITE THE STUDENT TO OBSERVE THE SITUATION

Declarative language is a powerful tool for helping students notice contextual clues that they might have missed.

If a student is caught up in their own activity, a simple reminder of what other students are doing might give help fall back into the collective task:

> *I notice Michael is preparing his cue cards.*
>
> *I can see Abed and Li have started on the worksheet.*

Or if a student struggles to recognise social cues you might them spot these signals:

> *I saw Jazmin smiling, she must have liked what you said.*
>
> *The others are looking this way, I wonder if it is our turn?*

One particularly effective way to encourage students to scan their environment is to employ 'words related to your feelings or senses ...' (Murphy, 2020, p. 55).

> *The teacher **looks** frustrated.*
>
> *I'm **feeling** cold now without my jumper on.*
>
> *I **heard** your aide said something.*
>
> *I can **see** people handing in their test.*
>
> *I can **smell** cinnamon. I wonder if the cake is ready.*
>
> *I just **heard** the Mrs K's rallying call.*

I have found that using 'sense words' not only encourages the student to be more aware of contextual clues but also helps me be more self-conscious about the signals I take for granted that the student might simply be missing.

You can also use non-verbal cues to reiterate these invitations. You might turn to face one of the student's classmates to model that you are giving attention to what they are saying. Or gesture at a worksheet that has been handed out to other students.

Non-verbal cues are a low-demand way to help the student pick up signals they might have missed.

PROMPT A COLLABORATIVE APPROACH

As we have already noted, there are many situations where you will find yourself instructing students what to do:

You should do that next ...

The way you have to handle this is ...

If you are confused then look at a dictionary ...

However, this power dynamic – the authoritative teacher dictating what the student should do – is precisely the dynamic that demand-avoidant young people baulk at. Instead of talking to the student this way, try to emphasise that you are working together as partners:

Let's *think about what to do next ...*

We *might handle this by ...*

*This word is confusing **us** ...*

Alternatively, you might this encourage this collaborative approach by downplaying your role and encouraging the student to take the lead.

It is hard for a demand-avoidant student to have partnership with their teacher if they feel that you already have all the answers and each step is predetermined. Instead, signal that you are uncertain how to proceed.

There are a couple of approaches that work well in this regard.

You can explicitly state your lack of understanding or confusion about the task:

I don't know *what to do next ...*

I'm unsure *how to handle this ...*

I'm perplexed *by that word ...*

Or you can use a 'wondering' statement that 'invites (the student) to help you solve a problem' (Truman, 2021, p. 28).

I wonder how I am going to organise all these points into paragraphs ...

I wonder how I get an answer without using a calculator ...

I wonder how I could make that colour ...

Laura Kerbey, who frequently uses this technique with students, insists that these wonderings must be authentic: 'these must be genuine questions so that the learner and I can work together to find things out' (Kerbey & Fricker, 2023, p. 59). I'd qualify this advice: sometimes you may be genuinely wondering how to approach a problem but in other situations you may know the answer already – what needs to be authentic is your curiosity *in how the student* will approach the problem. Similarly, when you suggest you are unsure how to proceed or can't understand something you may be feigning your response – but the idea that you are keen to collaborate on a solution together is genuine.

This self-deprecating approach tends to cue the student into consider how they might approach the problem. It is telling that when they students do this *they* often use collaborative language:

Could we ...

Let's try ...

Give students enough space to have a meaningful role in their learning and they will be more likely to take on that role.

FOREGROUND CHOICE AND OPPORTUNITY

Providing students with choice is another way to develop this sense of student agency. Instead telling them what to do, you are encouraging them to take action on their own behalf.

One way to do this is to use qualifiers such as 'perhaps', 'might' or 'maybe' to make it clear to the student that you are raising options – rather than giving a direct instruction. This emphasises that it is their decision on how to proceed:

Sometimes *it works well to highlight the key quotes* ...

Perhaps *trying a different approach would work* ...

*We **might** move on to revision later ...*

***Maybe** looking at the success criteria again is next ...*

Using cognitive verbs in your declarative statements has a similar effect (Murphy, 2020). Employing words such as 'decide', 'think' or 'wonder' model to the student the importance of thinking through their options – without ever making them feel like the decision isn't theirs to make:

*Let's **decide** what to do next ...*

*I'm **thinking** what's an alternative strategy we could try ...*

*I wonder if you **know** how to proceed from here ...*

*I **imagine** the solution must be in the extract somewhere ...*

*I **forgot** which question you wanted to do next.*

Young people sometimes get stuck using the same narrow range of approaches. Indeed, research suggest that young people don't usually seek out alternatives when making decisions in a wide range of domains (Fischhoff, 1996, pp. 232–48). Simply telling a student a different approach to use won't necessarily work if the student is oppositional or defiant. It is better in these instances to cue students as to other choices they might make and let them initiate their own decision making process.

You can offer these options to students non-verbally. You might use gestures to mime out that there a couple of different places they could sit. Or you can present students with a couple of work options by placing the tasks on their desk without saying anything but leaving them to make a choice. 'Strewing' learning materials in front of students in this way is fairly common approach for working with demand avoidance in junior primary school but is effective for students of all ages. I have sometimes used this technique with senior students who are prone to work refusal: giving them two essay questions instead of the single one I have provided for the rest of the class and watch how – without prompting they have made a selection and quietly moved on with the task.

AVOID ABSOLUTE NEGATIVES

Demand-avoidant students often react badly to being told 'No'. To them being told that they cannot do something can feel like an aggressive imposition of the teacher's authority and a compromise of their independence. This can quickly lead to lead to conflict. You can use declarative language to soften the way you refuse student requests and deescalate this potential conflict.

Laura Kerbey has pointed out that when we 'No' teachers often mean something more qualified:

> We often use the word 'No' when we mean something else. We say 'No you can't go outside' when we mean 'You can go outside at breaktime which is in 30 minutes' or 'You can go outside if you take an adult with you' (Kerbey, 2023, pp 30-31).

She suggests that positively reframing your comment by focusing on these qualifications is effective way to avoid this trap. In this way, a command such as:

> *No, you can't use your iPad!*

Can become the gentler response:

> *Yes you can use it at the end of the day during free time.*

Or:

> *No, you cannot leave the classroom on your own.*

Might be rephrased as:

> *Yes, you can go the office, when your aide can take you there.*

As with many examples of declarative language, it can be hard to come up with these on the spot. However, with practice you will come to identify the kids of conditions that you can use to turn a 'No' into the kind of qualified 'Yes ...' that a demand-avoidant student might accept.

STATE YOUR OWN APPROACH

Another way to support these students is to flag your own intended actions. You do this by clearly stating your intentions with personal pronouns:

> *I'm going to start the lesson now.*
>
> *My idea is to rewrite the notes on a study sheet.*
>
> *I will check my spelling at the end of the story.*

Telling a student how you will respond to a classroom situation or learning task offers them a model approach that they might choose to emulate.

Moreover, this approach sets clear boundaries between you and your student. It helps communicate that you have agency too. Remember you are trying to avoid telling them what to do – but endorsing their autonomy should not undermine yours. Afterall, saying what you intend to do is not placing a demand on them.

If you have a student who is overstepping the mark or even trying to manipulate you, framing declarative statements in this way might help you more clearly separate your needs and theirs.

Putting declarative statements into action

You may feel like declarative statements are unlikely to work – particularly if you are employing them for the first time or with a student who is normally very oppositional. Will it really help to tell the student that their 'book is closed' instead of instructing them to 'open their book?' Won't they just respond with 'so?'

The short answer is yes they may.

Remember though this strategy is typically used with students who are being demand-avoidant and if telling them just do something would work, you would have already tried that approach. What you want to do is to trial this technique and see if it has a better outcome than your traditional approach.

Carefully constructing your declarative statements using the tips above is one of the ways you do this – but there are some other pieces of advice you need to keep in mind.

WORD YOUR STATEMENTS CAREFULLY

Make sure phrase your statement precisely as you planned to deliver it. Sometimes teachers will carefully construct a statement and then deliver an approximation of what they planned to say that is not actually a declarative statement:

> Planned: *I noticed you did a second draft of your last story …*
>
> Delivered: *When will you revise this as a second draft?*

In this example, the teacher has rephrased the statement as a question. This is a common trap (Murphy, 2020.) Obviously, the sentiments are very similar but questions are usually more demanding than statements. Be mindful of small alterations of phrasing that might undermine the effect of what you are trying to do.

Be cognisant too of what language you use. Declarative statements have to prompt reflection and this won't happen if the vocabulary is pitched above the student's head or is so simple as to seem patronising. When I do video reviews of declarative statements that don't work, I have found that in more than half of the cases the teacher, on reflection, felt that the language that they used didn't match the student's ability. Target your word choice to the student's point of need so that they can easily reflect on what you've said.

KEEP PRACTISING

It will take time to feel comfortable using declarative statements. Using a declarative where you would typically use an imperative can feel counter intuitive. As a result, your delivery of even the most carefully constructed phrase can be stilted or awkward:

> Your. Book is. Closed.

Don't let this discourage you from using this technique. Sometimes, a declarative statement will work even if it is delivered with a wooden inflection or a halting tone. Moreover, if you keep using them, the fluency of your delivery will quickly improve. Keep practising the technique and it will come to feel more intuitive – and be more effective.

BE AWARE OF YOUR NON-VERBALS

It is not just your phrasing and delivery of which you need to be mindful. As with all verbal encounters with students, you are communicating not just with your words. Make sure your expression is calm. You want to demonstrate relaxed body language and use open handed, non-threatening gestures. Make sure you don't seem inpatient (no repeated glances at the unfinished task, furious foot tapping or looking over at the clock). In no way do you want to seem like you are pressuring them to follow an instruction. Instead your demeanour should communicate your genuine interest in what *they choose* to do next.

EXTEND YOUR WAIT TIME

Don't rush. After you deliver a declarative statement, make sure you offer the student extended take-up time. Remember most of the power of a declarative statement comes from giving the student a chance to notice something they might have missed and encouraging them to make an *informed* decision on how to act next. Students need time to process this information.

Sometimes it helps to busy yourself elsewhere in the class, working with another student, during this take up time. This both signals to the student the choice about how to proceed is really up to them – and makes it easier for you to refrain from jumping in with further directives.

This approach can work even if you don't then engage with other students. Pick a spot when you are not looking straight on at the student, but stand where you can watch the student you are helping through your peripheral vision. Note their initial response to what you've said: did it seem like it may have impact on their typical response? They may not immediately comply but if they don't respond with outright resistance the statement may already be subtly shifting the dynamic of your standard interactions.

Keep observing them. Do you start to see small flickers of engagement? Are there signs that, with a bit more wait time, they might re-engage with the task? Does the student pause what they are doing? Do they glance at the board or glance at their own work or another student? Don't be thrown if a student doesn't immediately respond to your declarative suggestion – be patient and you might find that your delivery was more successful than you realised.

BE AWARE OF CONTEXT

One of the challenges of working with a demand-avoidant student is that an approach that will work one day might not the next. You need to be conscious that demands can have a cumulative effect. If a student has had a lot of as demands placed on them, then an instruction you give that they are normally fine with might suddenly feel overwhelming to them.

It is useful here to draw a distinction between what the student can do (their capability) and what they are able to do at that moment (their capacity.) A student may have the *capability* to deal with a particular demand but not the *capacity* to deal with it given how they are currently feeling.

You won't always know when a student is about to reach their capacity. However, you can presume there will be times when they will. Keep this in mind when working with demand-avoidant students. Be on the lookout for situations both in and outside of class that might add to the volume of demands they face. Anticipate that sometimes you will need to be particularly careful about framing instruction in declarative terms – because the student has already reached the absolute limit of demands they can face.

Anticipate too that even if this sensitive approach is properly executed, it may still fail because of the context in which it was delivered. When you evaluate your use of declarative language, consider not just *what* you said and *how* you said it but *when* it was delivered and *how the student* might have been feeling when it was.

BE TARGETED

You will not be able to use declarative statements in all situations – nor should you. There are moments in a classroom when commands are necessary: you don't need to twist 'don't throw that javelin' into 'I'm noticing how pointy that is …'

The key idea to keep in mind here is that you are using declarative language to create a 'low-demand' environment – not a 'no-demand' environment. In a classroom or the yard there will always be situations where you have to set limits. As with any other student, young people who are demand-avoidant need limits that ensure their safety and the positive learning experience of their classmates.

The student doesn't have to be happy about these limits or even agree with you about them As Murphy is at pains to point out: 'learning to manage uncomfortable emotions is a vital part of resilience and growth' (Murphy, 2021).

You might though be able to soften the imposition of these limits by using declarative language. For example, you can use it to establish them in the first place:

> *It is important that your hair is tied up near the lathe.*
>
> *Other people will feel unsafe if we throw sticks.*

Or it can be employed to foreground an imperative instruction with some context:

> *It is important that your hair is tied up near the lathe. Tie your hair up.*
>
> *Other people will feel unsafe if we throw sticks. Put that down, thank you.*

Of course, no matter how well you use declarative statements there will always be situations where students baulk at being given limits. Indeed, whenever I use these statements I try to envisage what pivot phrase I might have to employ if they don't work. ('It's my job to decide what is safe in the classroom ...'). (See Pivoting – Chapter 4)

Remember though that even if they did not work in this particular instance – using declarative statements might have a positive effect in aggregate. Reducing the total number of demands you make though will mean that when you do have to firmly reiterate a command in the future that may you have some advantages:

- Your instruction will have extra weight because it is rare. You should only use absolute language when absolutely necessary: 'musts and nevers should be saved for non-negotiable rules' (Truman, 2020, p. 26). If the student feels like you are constantly putting demands on them, then an imperative is just one of many. If you rarely use direct instruction, then when you do the student is more likely to see the urgency and importance of your request.

- It's also likely that you will have stronger relationship with the student because there have been less moments of contention between you in past lessons. Stone and Heen (2014) found that strength of relationship is one of the most important triggers for determining whether someone takes up your feedback. If you have largely avoided getting into conflicts over demands in the past, you may be able to draw on the strength of the relationship you have built up with the student to ask them to follow your instruction on this occasion.

However, even if they aren't successful in this way, using these phrases will at least remind you that your goal in the classroom is not getting students to comply with *your* instructions but engage with *their* learning.

Conclusion

It takes finesse to decide how and when to use of low-demand instructions. When I coach teachers on using these techniques, I emphasise the importance of being deliberate:

- Are you being self-conscious about your choices or are you letting habit or circumstance dictate your instruction?
- Would your imperative instruction work better if you reframed it as a declarative statement?
- Are your style of instructions working well with this particular student?
- Would your declarative statement actually be more effective as an imperative command?

This self-consciousness is crucial because it reminds us to concentrate on the nuances of our practice rather than the student's limits. When just giving a student a simple instruction is tricky, it is easy to be overwhelmed by the extent of the problem. ('How can I get them learning when even asking them to sit in their seat is an issue?') Instead, focus on what you can control: the subtleties of your own craft. This is one of the greatest benefits of learning how to use declarative statements: they foster a greater sense of agency in your students – but also in you.

Chapter 4
Pivoting

> Sitting down was the issue – I was determined everyone was going to do it first, then I'd talk. Piston remained standing. I reordered. He paid no attention. I pointed out that I was talking to him. He indicated he heard me. I inquired then why in hell didn't he sit down. He said he didn't want to. I said I did want him to. He said that didn't matter to him. I said do it anyway. He said why? I said because I said so. He said he wouldn't. I said, 'Look I want you to sit down and listen to what I'm going to say.' He said he was listening. 'I'll listen but I won't sit down.'
>
> James Herndon, *How to survive in your native land,* 1971

This account was written by a teacher over fifty years ago, but when I read it to teachers now it still resonates with them. It is easy in teaching to find yourself in these sorts of farcical exchanges. Often you work out what you should have said long after these arguments have ended. In French, this is called staircase wit (l'esprit de l'escalier): the clever thing you think to say as you leave a situation. Indeed, coming up with the right thing to say in the middle of a fractious encounter with a student is sometimes very difficult. The danger is that when you argue with students, you end up in 'the gradual crescendo of improvised castigation' (Dix, 2017, p. 93).

There is a simple answer to this issue though: don't ad lib. The surest way to be able to react in the moment to defiant or aggressive student behaviour is to rehearse the approach you will take before these encounters occur. This is a particularly valuable approach when students are resisting verbal instruction. Anticipating how students commonly express resistance and practising how to respond will go a long way to building your capacity and confidence for resolving conflict in the classroom.

> The surest way to be able to react in the moment to defiant or aggressive student behaviour is to rehearse the approach you will take before these encounters occur.

The key thing you need to practise are pivot phrases.

Pivot phrases

Pivot phrases are 'rehearsed responses that lay out the precise language you can use to address a student who is being argumentative' (Pearsall, 2020, p. 26). There are four basic types of pivots: those that partially agree, redirect, reframe and acknowledge. In a single encounter with a student, you might end up using phrases from each of these types of pivots, but we will explore them one at time so you can get a better sense of which phrase works best with which particular aspect of a student's response.

PARTIAL AGREEMENT

Sometimes the easiest way to counter a student's argument is to agree with it. Students get used to teachers meeting their resistance with counterarguments. What they don't anticipate is that you might agree with what they are saying. By partially agreeing with what they have said, you can pivot around the disputed part of the exchange and concentrate on what you want them to do next.

> *It wasn't just me who wasn't in their seat!*
>
> **Perhaps not, but now everyone is clear on what my expectations are. Sit down, thank you.**
>
> *I didn't do it!*
>
> **Maybe you didn't, so open your book and get back to it, thanks.**

> Sometimes the easiest way to counter a student's argument is to agree with it.

This approach is a kind of compromise. You are not directly contesting what the student is saying, so they are more likely to feel heard. However, you are only partially agreeing. You are not saying they should continue with their current behaviour. This approach is a gentle way to briefly acknowledge the validity of the student's concerns and then guide them back to their work.

This technique is such a powerful pivot because it is built on the way students quickly learn the contours of familiar arguments and get adept at prosecuting them. Partially agreeing then 'wrong foots' these expectations. Indeed, I have used this technique several times with students who were so surprised that I actually agreed that they kept arguing – only to stop mid-sentence when they suddenly realised what was said.

Try partial agreement in your class and see if it shakes up patterns of how your students argue in the same way.

REDIRECTION

The basic form of this pivot is that you politely signal that what the student is arguing is not relevant to their current learning and refocus their attention on their studies.

'That's not the issue right now ...' is a classic example of a redirection pivot (Mackay, 2006). This is such an effective phrase. 'In six short words it manages to be both assertive (that's not the issue) and respectful (it might be the issue at another time but not *right now*) and can be used in a wide range of situations' (Pearsall, 2020, p. 28).

However, there are many other phrases that you can use in a similar way. 'That's not our concern at the moment', 'Let's focus on the task' and 'That's not our current priority' are all effective and versatile question stems:

> *Does anyone in here even like statistics?*
>
> **That's not our concern at the moment, Sam.**
>
> *I am so annoyed about lunchtime – I don't want to do this!*
>
> **Let's focus on the task, Lucinda.**
>
> *Can't you just let me play my game?*
>
> **Heidi, that's not our current priority. Back to your work, thank you.**

I also like to use a variation of this approach where you register what the student has said with a brief placeholder response and pivot straight back into your instruction. Paul Dix (2017) suggests 'Be that as it may …' is a good generic version of this style of pivot. I use 'Nevertheless …' in a similar way, but 'All that being said …' and 'Nonetheless …' are also effective. These short, sharp redirections work particularly well when a student is exhibiting low-level defiance or presenting you with a laundry list of reasons why they can't get back on task:

> *Can you get started on your work now, Adrienne?*
>
> *There are so many problems to do. I don't really like algebra, and I'm never going to use this in the future anyway.*
>
> *Nevertheless, get started on your work, thank you.*

When I coach teachers to use redirection pivots, they are often surprised at how they reduce long arguments to brief exchanges. Take some time to hone this approach and you might find that you have a similar experience.

REFRAMING

Rather than argue with a student on their terms, sometimes it is better to recast the argument itself.

> Rather than argue with a student on their terms, sometimes it is better to recast the argument itself.

One of the most common traps teachers fall into when dealing with resistance is they let the student decide what the issue is. You might want to discuss the student's choices or how their behaviour is affecting others but instead find yourself trying to defend yourself against the charge that you are picking on them or aren't treating everyone fairly. So frequently do I see this in classroom observations that I have a rough list of the four most common ways that students highjack conversations.

- **Personalisation:** You end up trying to explain why you don't have a personal grievance against the student.
- **Denial:** You end up arguing over what should be the uncontested facts about what actually took place that led to your encounter.

- **External attribution:** You have to discuss what others are doing in the room and what they are responsible for instead of focusing on the student's personal actions.
- **Becoming emotive:** You have to manage the student's emotional reaction to the situation rather than get to discuss their actions.

Reframing pivots give you a way to steer arounds these traps by redefining what you are talking about.

Temporary redirection

Whenever a student is trying to personalise an issue, I use this pivot:

Of course, you'd tell me off – you hate me!

I'm not talking about who you are – I'm talking about what you're choosing to do.

I have used this in many different situations: with students who are adamant I have a grudge against them, with those who throw a temper tantrum rather than face their own responsibilities, and whenever groups of students suggest I am singling them out. This pivot and phrases like it ('I'm talking about how you chose to act', 'I'm commenting on your actions not you') are versatile and should be an essential item in your teacher toolkit.

Statement of value

Another useful technique is making a so-called statement of value. For example, when students are claiming you are playing favourites or not treating everyone equally, I suggest responding like this:

Why does Mohammed get skip this exercise? I'm not doing it if he isn't!

I am fair to everyone. I don't treat you identically, though, because you are not identical.

This pivot is so effective because it recognises the presumption that underlies the student's comment – you have to treat everyone exactly the same to be fair – and directly challenges it. You are restating precisely how you view the situation.

Or to look at another example: if a student begins to deny some of the basic facts about their actions, for example, I will cut them off like this:

I won't debate what I saw, but I am happy to discuss how to resolve this problem.

Or if they try to argue that unsafe behaviours aren't dangerous:

> *It is my job to decide what is unsafe, and that behaviour is unacceptable.*

I find that sometimes you can even set up these pivots before the students speaks. When I want to discuss a student's behaviour with them, I usually say that I want to discuss a 'pattern of behaviour'. If they are contesting one example of what took place, you can then respond using a pivot like this: 'I am not talking about any one incident. I am talking about a pattern of behaviour.'

There are lots of variations of this pivot ('I don't treat you all the same because you don't all have the same needs') and many reframing pivots that challenge presumptions in this way. I was in a classroom recently where a teacher used three such pivots in the one exchange with a gifted Year 5 student:

> *You just ignored me and …*
>
> **There twenty-six students in the room, and I have to share out my time.**
>
> *Don't interrupt me!*
>
> **Conversations sometimes overlap, but I always wait until I have heard my students out. Okay?**
>
> *Anyway, why do I have to do this task? That group doesn't even have to write an essay! That's not fair.*
>
> **I differentiate tasks so they suit each individual student. Your task suits you; their task suits them.**

You may not be able to reel off these pivots as quickly as this, but learning a range of phrases for reframing discussion will make it easier to address students who are trying to define the terms of your discussion. The key to reframing an argument is being decisive. Act quickly to define the boundaries of the argument. Don't, goes my standard advice to teachers, accept the student's premise. Decide what the primary issue is and remain focused on this point throughout your encounter. If a student still tries to set up a different premise, simply use a micro command ('Not here', 'Not negotiable') and then repeat what you have said.

Be firm about what is acceptable to discuss, and you will be able to recast many debates so that they are more productive.

ACKNOWLEDGING

Sometimes you want to signal to the student that you have understood the feelings behind their argument before you pivot them back to what they should be doing. This is especially true in situations where emotions are high.

So much of the teacher–student conflict that occurs in the classroom has nothing to do with your teaching but is the product of the student's own context. (I always tell new teachers that when a student is getting very upset with them it usually isn't personal.) They might have trouble regulating their emotions, be dealing with the consequences of trauma or be struggling with a difficult home life. Perhaps they are just having a really bad day.

It is actually very impressive sometimes how much resilience some students show – despite the challenges they face – in just getting to school. If we treat these students as though they live in a vacuum, we are denying their reality. No wonder that sometimes our efforts to address their behaviour actually make them even more fractious.

An acknowledgement pivot can go a long way to addressing this issue.

Active listening

The simplest form of this pivot is to use some active listening:

> *I am angry that you are making me do this again!*
>
> **You are frustrated that I have asked you to draft your work. You need a final copy to complete this task, though.**

Explaining someone's view back to them is one of the most effective ways to acknowledge what they are thinking and feeling.

Signal empathy

Another simple form of this pivot is to offer the student a brief statement of understanding before you redirect them to their studies:

> *I am so annoyed we have to do this.*
>
> **I understand. Head over to your group, thanks.**

> *I hate having this class on Friday afternoon.*
>
> **I hear you. Let's get this done quickly.**

> *I get angry every time I have to do this.*
>
> **Okay. Try doing the first part, and I will check back in with you.**

Your approach is everything here. Use a warm, empathetic tone. Pause after the pivot statement to make sure the student registers your acknowledgement (I know . . .) and then offer your redirection with a friendly expression that suggests an offer of support (. . . so let's get started on this).

Agreement

You might go a step further and actually agree with what the student is saying. Sometimes this takes the form of the kind of partial agreement we discussed earlier:

> *I was going fine until you started to hassle me.*
>
> **Well, that may be so. You can get back to it now.**

Or perhaps you might employ a less qualified agreement like 'I've wondered that too' or 'I think something similar'. Chip and Dan Heath (2013) have noted that agreeing with someone – even going to the point of offering them extra reasons to support their argument – is a disarming way to address resistance in adults. This has certainly been my experience with young people. It is a powerful form of modelling to show students that you have some of the same feelings and concerns but nonetheless think focusing on the task is the best way to proceed.

It is effective to use acknowledgement when the discussion is heated. If students are aggressively asserting their authority, I will usually just agree with them. This helps foreground their authority and tends to de-escalate the situation:

> *You can't make me!*
>
> **You're right. No one can force you to complete this task. It is up to you.**
>
> *I don't have to do this if I don't want to!*
>
> **That's correct. You can choose whether to do it or not. It will be your decision if you do it.**

All of the examples I have included here are relatively brief exchanges, but acknowledgement pivots work well in longer interactions. Here is a good example from a classroom:

> *How could I do it if I can't even go to Dad's place because he is so pissed off with me? (Shouting) Am I meant to break into my house to steal my stupid homework? Am I meant to pick the locks? Smash a window?*

> *I understand. I can hear that this is a hard situation because of what happened. It might be true that you can't get it, but you could describe what you wrote. Sit here, and when you are ready we will talk about your contention.*

If you find these strategies effective, you might also want to investigate open responses and mistaken goal prompts, which are even more sophisticated versions of these acknowledgement pivots (see Chapter 4).

Conclusion

Pivoting, like many classroom skills, is a 'volume business'. You get better at it the more you do it. Teachers develop this skill in fits and starts as they respond to incidents that pop up in their classroom. This can take years of trial and error. Devoting dedicated time to working on how you defuse arguments or redirect off-task behaviour accelerates this natural process of skill acquisition.

At first, using these pivots might not feel natural. ('It worked,' one teacher told me of a pivot I suggested she use, 'but it felt like ventriloquism.') However, if you put in the time, you will feel yourself becoming more comfortable with using them quite quickly.

Once you are more at ease using pivots in your class, be proactive and try to actively seek out student arguments for which you don't have a ready answer. This is, in my experience, the trademark of teacher who is highly accomplished at pivoting: they plan ahead and are constantly on the lookout for pivots they can add to their repertoire.

I often tell the story of a teacher who I worked with very early in my coaching career whose students routinely told her that her class was 'boring'. She couldn't find a suitable response to this. Tactically ignoring the students only encouraged them to say it more often, and directly contesting them didn't work:

> *This is boring.*
>
> **No, it's not.**
>
> *Yes, it is. How can you tell me what I think?*

Nor did any of my usual responses. ('Be that as it may' and 'Nevertheless' clearly weren't the right approach.)

At the same school where she worked, I observed a teacher who had a deft way of dealing with this problem. She responded to a student saying her class was boring by telling him, 'I welcome feedback. Just not at the start of the session. We can discuss my performance after the class if you would like.' The teacher I was working with quickly adopted this phrase in her classes. As did I.

Taking particular notice of what students say that you don't have a response to makes you more alert to these moments.

However, there is another advantage to focusing on the gaps in your list of pivots – and indeed pivots more generally. It helps makes these encounters feel less personal. Instead of being caught in an individual exchange, you are looking at *patterns* of student argument. Trying to identify *types* of resistance in this way gives you some emotional distance and, if you find a potential solution, a response you might use in lots of other situations.

Explore the pivots we have discussed here and see if they create a similar shift of mindset in your practice.

Chapter 5
Talking it out

Addressing complex behavioural issues is a marathon not a sprint, and it is unrealistic to think that we can turn around a student's behaviour in a single exchange. Using a pivot might circumvent an argument, but it will not instantly alter established habits or fix poor practices.

It takes time, after all, to build a relationship with a student, address their underlying learning issues and put in place institutional support to reduce the risk factors that adversely shape their experience of school. A good deal of this work is done at a whole-school level and actually takes place over years. However, you still need everyday strategies for dealing with off-task behaviour while you wait for these longer-term approaches to take effect.

Sometimes nudging and reminding, giving instructions, and pivoting don't work. When this is the case, teachers tend to fall back on 'talking it out' – one-on-one discussions where you unpack the issue with the student and seek their commitment to change their behaviour. This might include everything from a quiet exchange at the student's desk through to a lengthy discussion with them at the end of class that runs into recess.

In my experience, schools usually have formal processes for teacher–student meetings and behavioural conferences but devote less thinking to how to get the most out of these more informal discussions. It is worth spending some time thinking about how best to conduct these one-on-one encounters because – like any skill – we can get better at these conversations with practice. This chapter will explore some well-established strategies you can use to do this.

Foregrounding choice

You are not the person who ultimately changes your student's behaviour. They are. Talking it out is then not about telling the student what to do but seeking their assistance to shift their behaviour.

> You are not the person who ultimately changes your student's behaviour. They are.

One of the most effective ways to discuss behaviour change with a student is to encourage them to take ownership of this change. Change is a radically different process when it is not being done *to you* but rather it is something *you choose* to do. This is as true for teachers as much as it is for students. If you are *told* to adopt a technique during professional learning, the likelihood that you will actually do it is quite low. Whereas if, during a coaching conversation, you *decide* to do something, the take-up rate is radically higher (Joyce & Showers, 2002). The challenge then is finding quick ways to remind students of their autonomy.

COLLABORATION SIGNALS

One of the most overlooked ways to foreground choice is to ask the student for their help.

This technique is particularly useful for when you draw a student aside to talk with them about their behaviour. These encounters can make students uneasy – which is often evident in the way they adopt defensive body language as they are approached or called to the front of the room. This defensiveness is even more pronounced when the student is asked to stay behind to talk with the teacher.

To address this unease, start your discussion by thanking them for their time:

> *Thanks for letting me interrupt you.*
> *Thank you for staying back to talk with me.*

This cues the student that this will be a positive interaction – you are not angry or going to be aggressive. Teachers often skip this step. Remember, though, our motto is 'relationship first, task second', so take a moment to send a clear signal about your constructive intent.

You then reiterate this message by asking for the student's support:

I think you could help me with something ...

I need your assistance ...

I need your help clarifying an issue that occurred in class today ...

This approach is disarming because it frames the rest of the conversation with the student as a help-seeking discussion (Lewis, 2008). Again, you often see the impact of this approach in their body language: the student – all crossed arms and tightly coiled posture – visibly relaxing when instead of being levelled with an accusation they receive an invitation to help out.

The simple act of asking students for their help means that they are more likely to be an active agent in these discussions.

THE LANGUAGE OF CHOICE

Another thing you can do to encourage student agency is to make a conscious decision to highlight that behaviour is a choice. At every opportunity, try to remind students that a significant determinant of what happens in their school life will be the sum total of their choices. There is no one script for doing this; rather you have to make a concerted effort to foreground the role of choice whenever you are discussing off-task behaviour:

You can make a better choice ...

If you made a poor decision, you can fix it by ...

If you elect to address the impact of your behaviour ...

Choose a better option, thank you ...

Using this language in one-on-one discussions emphasises that you are not talking about the student's character but their actions. ('I'm not talking about who you are but what you are choosing to do.')

Indeed, a number of unproductive behaviours that are common in one-on-one discussions seem to occur less when you seed your conversation with this emphasis on choice. I noticed in my own teaching, for example, that students who in the past would sitting sullenly through a meeting without making eye contact or saying much were suddenly much more active in one-on-one meetings. Similarly, students of mine who had tried to avoid real reflection – nodding their head rapidly as I approached them and eagerly declaring this will never, ever happen again, and can I go now please – were much more reflective when I routinely used this technique.

Using the language of choice conveys to students a powerful idea: poor behaviour is really just poor decision-making and can be fixed by better decision-making.

> Using the language of choice conveys to students a powerful idea: poor behaviour is really just poor decision-making and can be fixed by better decision-making.

DIRECTED CHOICE

You can even use this approach when one-on-one conversations are heated. If a student is being resistant or even defiant, you simply offer them two courses of action for changing their behaviour and let them choose which course of action they'd like to follow:

Magda, close your laptop or turn it so it faces me. It is up to you.

Amara, either move over to the group at the back or sit with these guys here. You decide which you prefer.

You can either complete the essay work or start on the notes. Those are your two options.

The great advantage of this approach is that you are giving a firm instruction but preserving the student's sense of agency. Young people's lives are heavily proscribed by the authority of others: teachers, parents or carers, and all of the other adults who have power over them. It is easy to forget sometimes just how often students are told what to do. Especially if you are a student who finds it hard to self-regulate your behaviour and so need lots of correction. Giving students the chance to make an informed choice about their behaviour then is both a powerful motivator and a way to encourage them to take responsibility for their actions.

However, you need to be careful using this technique, as directed choices are often misunderstood and misapplied. The potential trap here is that you don't actually offer the student a choice so much as a thinly veiled threat:

Put that away or you can go the principal's office. It's your decision.

You can finish that now or stay in with me at lunch time and do it then.

These sorts of comments do not provide the student with a meaningful choice. Moreover, students who are angry or exhibit oppositional defiance will sometimes deliberately take up the least preferred of these options as a way of showing you their independence (which is inconvenient if you really just wanted that lunch break). Of course, there is nothing wrong with making clear to students the potential consequences of their actions, but if you really want them to have more of a feeling of autonomy, this is not the way to go about it.

Directed choices need to consist of two genuine options. However, coming up with these options takes practice, so before you initiate this strategy, take a moment to consider the choice you are putting to the student: Are they real options? Could the student legitimately pick either? Are they, roughly speaking, equally appealing?

Offer the directed choice in a calm, matter-of-fact tone and then move away from the encounter to emphasise that what happens next is up to the student. Avoid any hesitancy such as lingering or looking back to check what the student is going to do. You want to give the impression that you expect the student to make a good choice without close supervision.

Don't rush here. Give the student time to consider their options. You may need to wait for them to calm down or the interest of their peers to wane before they are ready to comply. Watch the student through your peripheral vision. Is there any sign that they are getting back to work? If after a few minutes they still have not made a choice, prompt them with some proximity or a collective progress check (see Chapter 1) to see if you can nudge them into taking up one of the options.

If this doesn't work, you can use an individual progress check. The most effective way to do this is just to offer another directed choice:

Have you decided yet, or do you need more time?

This phrase is carefully worded to both prompt the student and to reiterate their sense of autonomy. Anticipate that sometimes it is at this point in the encounter when the student's temper will flare. Typically, by this stage the student has seen that you are prepared to doggedly insist that they take responsibility for their actions, so the function of this behaviour is to attempt to push you away. Do not be deterred. Reiterate that how they act is their choice ('Sounds like you need more time') and give them one last opportunity to take up your offer.

A directed choice is a highly effective strategy, but nothing works every time. If the student still doesn't comply, this is the time to move to a more formal, school-level response to the behaviour. Make sure that even as you do this you use the language of choice – a final reminder that the student is choosing this consequence and could be making better choices.

Focusing on choice helps you be assertive without being authoritarian. It puts the onus on students to take responsibility for their actions, teaching them to 'manage their own behaviour and ... anticipate consequences' (Mackay, 2020, p. 44). Focusing on choice helps you meet the key goals of talking it out: getting the student to change their problematic behaviour while maintaining a positive relationship with them.

> Focusing on choice helps you be assertive without being authoritarian. It puts the onus on students to take responsibility for their actions.

Saving face

Consider the following maths problem:

A bat and a ball cost $1.10 in total. The bat costs $1 more than the ball. How much does the ball cost?

What is your answer? We will return to this problem in a moment ...

It is one of the most common traps in one-on-one discussion to treat everything the student has done as a considered decision. Of course, this does not always reflect how students actually make their choices. In the last twenty years, there has been an entire body of research that has shown that human decision-making is predictably irrational (Wilkinson & Klaes, 2018). We are impulsive, prone to all sorts of cognitive biases and driven by rough, rule of thumb mental shortcuts (Kahneman, 2011).

I often demonstrate this in workshops by using the maths problem at the start of this section. The correct response is five cents (the ball costs $0.05 and the bat $1.00 more than the ball at $1.05, giving a total of $1.10), but a large majority of people's answer to this question is ten cents. This is because, when analysing this sort of problem, the brain takes a kind of cognitive shortcut to estimate the answer.

Interestingly, if you were able to correctly answer this problem, your initial response may have still been ten cents. It is just that you have learned to account for the impulsive nature of first thoughts – to check over your work. Most of the research initially done in this field focused on adults, but clearly children are prone to the same biases. However, as a teacher, it is easy to see that young people might struggle even more with a question like this, as they have had less time to develop the kind of reflective strategies that help you avoid error here.

This is broadly true of most of the problems that young people face; they are simply newer to the world and are only just learning how to cope with their own impulses and emotions. When issues arise in the classroom, it is your role to provide the student with the opportunity to better reflect on their choices. At some fundamental level, this is the primary purpose of one-on-one discussion: you are giving your students an opportunity to reconsider their actions, think about the impact they have on others and recognise patterns of behaviour.

> Young people ... are simply newer to the world and are only just learning how to cope with their own impulses and emotions.

However, sometimes you need to do this not just at the macro level of the discussion but for individual things they say or do. When a student does something inappropriate, take a moment before you respond to ask yourself: was this a considered action or were they behaving impulsively? I often put this question to teachers this way: would the student repeat that behaviour if you gave them a second chance?

FACE-SAVING CUES

The simplest way to do this is to offer your students a face-saving cue. These are brief prompts encouraging them to make a better choice:

Do you want to replay that?

There are lots of situations where face-saving prompts are applicable. The student might have used inappropriate or inflammatory language:

The principal is an idiot.

Do want to try that again?

Or acted out impulsively:

I'll let you reconsider that choice.

Or just said or done something that you think they will come to regret – and you want to give them a chance to quickly make it right before you have to initiate a serious (and time-consuming) response:

Did you really mean for that to happen?

These responses are a great way to reframe a potentially explosive situation or reset one that looks like it will become adversarial. Of course, there are ways to do this other than using a prompt. If a student does something inappropriate (and isn't interrupting their classmates' learning) you might choose – at first – to tactically ignore them in the hope that they will self-regulate their behaviour. Or perhaps you might initiate a longer discussion with a student where you point out why their behaviour was unrepresentative and remind them that they can make better choices:

I know that you are not someone who does hurtful things or uses put-downs. We are going to have a reset. I want you to tell me again how you feel and what I can do to help you.

The key here is not to dwell on what the student did wrong. (I had a colleague who used to say the main skill in face-saving was 'showing some tactical amnesia.') Use a calm, matter-of-fact tone to indicate that you don't want to get caught up in the student's initial response. Your manner should indicate you are not going to react to their provocations. You just want to them get back to the learning.

Students get better at taking up these opportunities the more you use them. Obviously, this is not always the case. In my last book, I mentioned an incident where I asked a student if he wanted a chance to replay what they said to me without shouting, and he responded by screaming a loud 'No!' in my face (Pearsall, 2020). Since that book was published a number of teachers have shared similar stories with me. Tellingly, though, they have all gone on to say that once the student was more familiar with this strategy, they readily took up the opportunity to walk back their poor choices.

Consider another maths problem:

There are water lilies on a lake. Each day, the amount of water lilies doubles. After forty-eight days, there are so many water lilies that the entire lake is covered. After how many days was half of the lake covered?

What is your answer? Again, we will return to this problem in a moment...

It makes sense that students get better at using these opportunities to reconsider their behaviour. This is how reflection works. We inevitably make mistakes but, with effort, get better at fixing them. Look at the maths problem. Most people's initial answer is to pick day twenty-four. The correct answer is day forty-seven. Many of you reading this would have initially got this wrong because humans find it hard to have an intuitive sense of how exponential growth works (Kahneman, 2011). However, after having done the bat and ball problem earlier, you are now more likely to be on the lookout for knee jerk answers that are incorrect. You still might not have got the right answer (we are innately wired to take cognitive shortcuts), but you were probably more wary of your initial response. This is a good analogy of how face-saving strategies help build a culture of reflection among your students.

By way of conclusion, it is worth mentioning why we call these strategies *face-saving*. They have this label because they aim to preserve the dignity of the student by separating them from their impulsive actions. When you use one of these strategies you are effectively saying to the student 'I am not going to judge you for your initial behaviour – I think you can show me a better version of yourself.' We don't, as teachers, want to be judged by our worst mistakes. We want people to see the sum of our actions and recognise our efforts to do our best. These face-saving strategies give you a quick, practical way to extend the same opportunity to your students.

Prompting reflection

A key goal of these conversations is that we want students to see their behaviour in a new light. One of the most effective ways to do this is to help the student separate the emotion they are experiencing and the actions that are driving this emotion. 'You can feel angry,' we often tell primary school students, 'but you don't have to act angry.'

There are two conversational scripts you can use to help students gain some distance from their own emotions: open responses and mistaken goal prompts. Both of these strategies take time to master but are worth the investment as they are particularly useful techniques to have when talking it out with angry and upset students.

OPEN RESPONSES

This is a script for giving students a chance to articulate what they are feeling. You offer the student a statement describing how you think they might be feeling and leave them space to respond to this assessment. Don't make this a long, detailed characterisation but a simple open-ended statement delivered in a soft empathetic tone. Here some of the examples:

You appear frustrated ...

You seem out of sorts ...

You sound a bit annoyed ...

The language might be simple here, but the delivery takes some finesse.

The crucial thing is refraining from adding further commentary after your statement. (The most important part of an open response is the ellipsis.) You want to create a space for the student express themselves – not offer another piece of advice from an adult that they are expected to follow. Even a brief pause will go a long way here. We often overestimate how long conversational silences actually go for; the average pause between speakers in conversation is only one two-hundredth of a second, so even a pause of a couple of seconds should be enough to generate a response (Stivers et al., 2009).

Anticipate that the student may use this opportunity to vent. ('There is often a lot of heat before there is any light' was how one sub-school coordinator summarised this to me.) Focus on listening to what they have to say without offering comment or advice. This can be hard – as teachers we are hard-wired to help young people – but just show you are available and ready to listen.

Anticipate too that sometimes your characterisation of their behaviour will be wrong. Or at least your student will tell you that it is wrong. ('I am not angry!') Don't be thrown by this. Acknowledge what they have said – some people will use active listening here to indicate they have heard the student, but I often just use a placeholder like 'okay' or 'alright' – and pause to see if the student wants to explain what they think is the issue.

Obviously, open responses don't work in every instance, but giving students encouragement to speak to their feelings can change how they are acting. Sometimes an open response provides a student with an opportunity to really reflect on their behaviour – and even problem-solve a situation. Other times it just gives them a chance to debrief. Either way, it is certainly worth trialling whenever a student's emotions are clouding their judgement.

MISTAKEN GOAL PROMPTS

You might also try helping the student make the connection between how they are feeling and how they are acting. The idea of a mistaken goal prompt is that you explicitly link the student's behaviour to its function. Typically, this is done in the form of a carefully posed question:

Did you just want to decide for yourself what to do?

Did you need me to come over?

Did you find it more interesting to do that than the task?

Student behaviour is logical. When a student repeatedly exhibits a particular behaviour, that behaviour usually has a function.

> Student behaviour is logical. When a student repeatedly exhibits a particular behaviour, that behaviour usually has a function.

However, this does not mean that the student is always aware of the function of the behaviour. Many behaviours have subconscious goals that drive them.

Offering your students this kind of prompt can help them appreciate their own motivations.

As with an open response, anticipate that often you will mischaracterise their motivation. Have a look at these examples taken from two high school settings:

> *Did you feel hurt and want them to feel hurt too?*
>
> No. I never meant it to hit them. I just threw it because I was bored, sir.
>
> *Did you want to avoid this exercise?*
>
> I thought you'd kick me out of class, and then [laughing] I thought I could use my phone.

In both of these examples the teacher has misread the situation, but this misreading has still led to a clearer picture of what is driving the student's off-task behaviour.

Of course, making the link between how a student feels and their actions is just the start of the conversation. It takes practice to conduct these conversations in a productive manner. Be on the lookout for the sub-skills that make this easier. I found, for instance, that using an acknowledgement pivot was a good technique for showing my students that I felt their goals were legitimate – even if the way they were going about reaching them was problematic:

> *Did you want to be the one to decide when you did this?*
>
> Yeah, I suppose.
>
> *I understand. I like to be independent too. Do you think you could find a way to do this without interrupting the others?*

I also found I got better at challenging students who were in denial about their emotional motivation when I was more aware of how I delivered these challenges. Softening my tone and adding more qualifiers was the key:

> [Angrily] I wasn't doing it to get attention.
>
> *I'm sure that wasn't the only reason, [much more quietly with a rising inflection] but I wonder whether you might have done it that second time so I would notice how angry you were?*

Mistaken goal prompts and open responses are a great way to initiate a discussion about emotions and, with practice, for unpacking fraught topics in a sensitive way. Use them regularly and you will find that not only will they help your students recognise what they are feeling and how their behaviour is driven by those feelings but also 'that a pattern of unacceptable behaviour is not the way to gain the sort of recognition and feelings of belonging that they really want' (Lewis, 2008, p. 105).

Restorative chat

Restorative justice is a powerful idea for resolving conflict in your class. It asks students who have done the wrong thing to consider the harm that they have done and then take responsibility for repairing the situation. Restorative justice puts a particular emphasis on hearing the voice of the victim *and* the perpetrator and eschews proforma punishments and empty apologies for meaningful resolutions to classroom issues.

> Restorative justice .... asks students who have done the wrong thing to consider the harm that they have done and then take responsibility for repairing the situation.

Schools that employ a restorative justice approach establish a wide array of formal processes to support teachers in this demanding task. However, even if your school uses a different framework and you don't have access to these formal processes, you might still be able to draw on the principles behind restorative justice when discussing issues with your students.

The simplest way to do this is to use a restorative chat. Sometimes known as an *impromptu conference*, this is a quick, informal discussion where you bring together students involved in conflict and get them to resolve the situation. My approach, which draws heavily on the work of Thorsborne and Vinegrad (2009), breaks this process into three steps: reflection, acknowledgement and repair.

REFLECTION

Take the students aside. Indicate immediately to the students that this is not going to be a conversation about blame ('No one is in trouble here ...').

I often use a collaboration signal (discussed earlier in this chapter) to convey that this will be a positive, solution-focused discussion.

Ask the student whose behaviour was problematic to consider what just happened. The phrasing of this question is crucial. There are two components to this. In the first half of the sentence, you offer a precise description of the off-task behaviour:

> *Louise, when you took Linda's book without asking ...*

This allows you to quickly establish the facts of the case, making clear to the student that they are uncontested and giving them no opportunity 'at all of denying what happened' (Thorsborne & Vinegrad, 2009, p. 44). Then you offer a reflection question:

> *... what were you thinking?*

Thorsborne and Vinegrad (2009) label this a 'thinking question' (p. 45). They suggest that phrasing it this way helps avoid the traps commonly associated with asking a student 'why' they did it (see Chapter 7).

If the student replies with an 'I don't know' or a very brief response, use some pause time to encourage them to elaborate. If you still get nothing, try the question a different way. I find that questions that focus on the function of the student behaviour work best:

> *What were you after when you did that?*
>
> *What did you think might happen?*
>
> *Could you talk me through your thinking?*

Now ask them to consider the other student or students' perspective:

> *What do you think they were feeling when this happened?*
>
> *How do you think they felt about what you did?*
>
> *How were your classmates affected by what took place?*

This cues to students that you are going to be looking at the impact of their behaviour from the perspective of others.

ACKNOWLEDGEMENT

Ask the student affected by the behaviour how they were impacted by it. If the affected student struggles to do this, ask some follow-up questions aimed at sounding out their immediate responses to the other student's behaviour:

What did you think when Tarwin did that?

How did it make you feel when this was happening?

Alternatively, Thorsborne and Vinegrad (2009) suggest that if the students struggle to answer, you can ask these questions of yourself:

Did you understand how this impacted me?

This provides a model for the other students but also reminds the off-task student that you are affected by what they do too.

This is important. One of the most common mistakes people make when using restorative justice is that they ignore the feelings of a very important stakeholder: themselves. Employing restorative justice should not be a test of personal endurance. For it to be effective, it can't rely on your own sense of altruism. Students must see that their actions have an effect on all of those around them, including you.

Moreover, you want them to see 'how to communicate with someone who disagrees with you' (Smith et al., 2015, p. 100). Include yourself in the process and be a model for calm dispute resolution.

Now ask the student what they have been thinking while hearing how their behaviour has affected others.

Tarwin, what were you feeling as we discussed this?

What could you say to Karl about this issue now?

Some schools call this the apology phase of the chat, making it compulsory at this point that the student says sorry both to their classmate and to their teacher. I am not sure about this label or indeed practice. I think it is actually easy to *say* sorry. We don't want our students thinking a lip-service apology is the way we resolve problems. Nor do we want to penalise those students who find it hard to show that they are sorry when they might be willing to demonstrate contrition in other ways.

Think instead of this as about acknowledgement. We just want, observes Ramon Lewis (2008), to 'get the student's agreement that there is a problem' (p. 83).

REPAIR

As the name suggests, restoring relationships that have been compromised in some way is at the heart of restorative practice. The repair phase is crucial to this. You need to get students thinking about how to resolve the problems between them. Starting with the affected student, seek out solutions:

> *How could Tarwin fix this problem?*

Your primary role here is to facilitate the discussion. This means both bouncing suggestions between the students ('Tarwin, do you think that would work?') and monitoring the practicality of their solutions. ('Do think you buying Karl lunch all week is fair or even affordable?')

Once students have a solution, close the discussion by setting a review date. This is a step I see busy teachers skip all the time. Don't make this mistake. Students need to know that it is not their words in the meeting but their actions afterwards that matter the most:

> *Okay, that sounds like a plan. I will check in at the end of the double to see if everyone has stuck to our agreement. Thanks for your time discussing this issue.*

There are of course other scaffolds you can use to map your conversations with students who have done the wrong thing. Ramon Lewis's (2008) nine-step protocol for discussing off-task behaviour is a practical and easy-to-adopt example that I have used frequently in my classes. However, I particularly like the restorative chat because its basic principles (reflect, acknowledge, repair) are at the heart of all of these conversations. Asking students to reflect on their actions, consider who has been affected and seek to repair the situation is not just a one-on-one meeting scaffold that you can use to unpack incidents with students – it is a framework for thinking about how we approach all our attempts at dealing with serious off-task behaviour.

Conclusion

When I started teaching, I had two strategies for dealing with serious off-task behaviour: the first was to yell ... and if that didn't work the second option was to yell louder. Talking with other more experienced teachers, though, I soon discovered that there was a host of more subtle interventions that I could use instead of this blunt force approach.

However, learning to talk it out with upset and defiant students was the area that took longest to develop any real confidence in my practice. This is understandable. These strategies require a great deal of patience and real dedication to nuance to learn, and it only takes one explosive encounter to make you feel you are back to square one.

With this in mind, approach the strategies in this chapter with realistic expectations. Be patient. Pick one strategy at a time. Identify a set of behaviours or mode of resistance that bothers you. Select a technique that might address this issue and trial it several times in your class. Find out who else at your school uses this technique successfully and seek out their advice. Make adjustments and try it some more. Whenever I am coaching someone through these strategies, I tell them that the key here is 'making quality mistakes'. That is, there is nothing wrong with failed attempts as long as you are alert to new approaches and constantly refining what you're doing.

Obviously, if these strategies don't change your students' behaviour, the next step is a formal, school-level intervention. If you do need to resort to this step – and sometimes this is absolutely the best way to support a student – then at least you can do so knowing you have given the student every opportunity to modify their own behaviour.

Chapter 6
Seeking support

I worked with a teacher who was being bullied by one of his students. This went on for weeks. The first I or his colleagues heard of it was when the teacher had to go on stress leave. When he returned to school, the teacher still couldn't believe he let it go on for so long: 'We had actually been doing a unit on bullying and bystander behaviour in that class and I still I didn't tell anyone.'

Seeking out help for something that is happening in your classroom is a socially complex moment. For some teachers, asking for help makes them feel vulnerable – like they are underperforming. Or they feel like it might compromise their relationship with student or send the wrong signal about their classroom authority to the young people they teach. Sometimes teachers feel like there is nothing that can (or will) be done about the persistently difficult behaviours of a particular student. Or they may be worried about the burden that sharing their issues will have on others. In my coaching conversations, teachers often tell me that they don't share their problems as much as they perhaps should because they are reluctant to add to the workload of already-busy colleagues.

Seeking out support can feel uncomfortable, but it is important that you understand that behavioural issues are something that should be addressed as a community. Students must understand that when you challenge their behaviour it is not personal. If a young person makes another student feel unsafe or interrupts the learning of their classmates, you have to address that behaviour not because you have a personal problem with it but because that behaviour is unacceptable in your learning community. If the students don't accept this message about communal expectations from you, you need to draw on the wider community to reiterate this message.

Strategies for seeking support

The form this community-level response takes will vary from school to school. Different schools have different frameworks for dealing with off-task behaviour, and the process you have to follow to seek out support will be different depending on which framework your school uses. As has been mentioned elsewhere in this book, I do not advocate any one particular framework for dealing with off-task behaviour. So rather than comment on the various processes you have to follow in your setting, I want to discuss some general principles you can bring to the – sometimes tricky – practice of asking for help.

MOVE QUICKLY

Endurance is overrated. Putting up with sustained bouts of difficult behaviour can substantially interfere with the learning of your students and can be incredibly stressful for you. Intervening early is the best way to help the student, their classmates and yourself.

> Endurance is overrated. Intervening early is the best way to help the student, their classmates and yourself.

If you are reluctant to initiate a formal process, at least do a *context check in*. This is a quick, informal chat where you mention to a coordinator or mentor that the student's behaviour is problematic and may require serious follow-up at some point in the future. This gives your colleague a heads up about the issue and means if you need to seek out further support from them, they have the context to act quickly in response. Moreover, this approach works well because it is low stakes (you are not yet asking for help) but are habituating yourself to sharing your concerns about your students.

In my experience, effective classroom managers have a bias to action. They are fast to respond to emerging issues, and their decisiveness means that they get to deal with these issues before they become entrenched. Acting quickly – even if it is just for a context check in – is a good way to adopt this mindset.

BE DESCRIPTIVE

Explain, in concrete terms, what is taking place. Avoid emotive language. You want the person to understand precisely what you are experiencing in class not just how you feel about it. This helps focus their attention on the underlying issue. You don't want them to dismiss the issue as your personal problem with a student. ('Amanda is struggling with Shane in 8E, but he is fine in my class.') Nor do you want them thinking you are just seeking reassurance. You are seeking a school-level response.

Sometimes being descriptive and dispassionate in this way is difficult. You may actually want to debrief about how the student's behaviour has emotionally impacted you. If this is case, just make sure the colleague you are speaking to knows that this is the purpose of the conversation. Tell them you are not after solutions or initiating a formal response – you just want someone to listen to you. Delineating between describing what the issue is and debriefing about how you feel about it means that when you do ask for help, your colleague knows how to best support you.

BE STRATEGIC

You also need to describe your response to the student's behaviour. This is an opportunity to flag the strategic nature of this response. If you are worried that mentioning you are struggling to deal with a student might undermine your standing in the school, being able to describe what you have tried so far signals two important things to your colleague. First, it lets them know that asking for help is a *considered* choice. You are not being forced into seeking out help because you are struggling but because you have trialled a number of classroom solutions but think a school-level response might now be more appropriate. I find listing the strategies you have trialled so far is a good way to do this:

> *I have tried using cross praise and other non-verbal strategies. ECA and some I statements haven't been effective yet, nor has our restorative chat. I'm just wondering whether we might try something now at the sub-school level.*

The use of *yet* is telling here because the other thing you are signalling is that you are open to suggestions. You are not saying nothing will work with this student just that nothing has worked so far. Being a professional means being always on the lookout for ways to refine your practice and framing your request for assistance in this way foregrounds this.

Rather than asking for help being a sign of weakness, it can be an opportunity to demonstrate your professional and strategic approach to classroom problems.

> Rather than asking for help being a sign of weakness, it can be an opportunity to demonstrate your professional and strategic approach to classroom problems.

TAKE RESPONSIBILITY

If you raise an issue at the school level, you need to make sure that you take an active role in whatever response is implemented to address this behaviour.

When I talk to coordinators and school leaders about behavioural issues, their primary complaint is that teachers 'handball' problems to them. That is, some teachers will bring an issue to them without offering any help themselves, expecting that it will be solved for them. This, of course, is unfair. If a set of behaviours is tricky enough to be raised at this level, possible solutions are unlikely to be instantaneous or implemented without any input from the classroom teacher. You need demonstrate that you are going to take share of responsibility for addressing the situation.

This is not just so you are being a good colleague – though this is part of it – but also because assigning responsibility to others means we never learn how we can change situations. The trap to avoid here is called *external attribution*. Challenging behaviour can be so confounding that you are tempted to blame someone else for the problem: colleagues, parents and carers, past teachers, the principal and so on. Do not make this mistake. Keep thinking about what you can do differently to help the student and shape their behaviour.

Be wary of those who give you the opposite message (especially would-be mentors). It is understandable if a colleague wants to sympathise with you being in a tricky situation, but you don't want them offering rationalisation for poor practice. Or worse, endorsing excuses you are making to yourself.

(My favourite rule of thumb for mentors is to find one that gives you what you need not what you want.) Don't separate yourself from the situation. It might be uncomfortable having to look at your own role in the issue but being actively involved in exploring the problem means you will be an active part of the solution too.

Conclusion

When I coach teachers on how to seek help, I always draw an analogy to their own students. 'When one of your students is in a difficult situation,' I ask, 'how do you want them to act?' Teachers invariably tell me they want their students to be unembarrassed about seeking help and to do it immediately when the need arises. When I press them about what, at their school, students have been taught to do to seek help, they talk about describing the problem, listening carefully to the helper's response and taking responsibility for putting in place the solutions that are offered. This is exactly what we need to do when we are seeking support.

Asking for help can be a confronting aspect of teaching but keeping these principles in mind – principles that we advocate to students all the time – can go a long way to making this an easier and more effective process.

Part 2
UNDERSTANDING ENTRENCHED OFF-TASK BEHAVIOUR

Chapter 7
What is the purpose of off-task behaviour?

The two whys

As a graduate teacher, I'd ask students who had done the wrong thing in my class to stay behind to discuss their behaviour. My standard approach to this conversation was to open it by asking them why they had misbehaved:

Why did you yell out like that?

Why did you ignore my instruction?

Why did you refuse to start the task?

The students' answers were rarely satisfying. There was lots of blame shifting and rationalisation but little insight. Of course, this is not surprising. In my entire career, I have never seen a student who was in a heightened state, be able to respond to 'Why did you do that?' in a reflective fashion:

I was engaged in classic stimulus-seeking behaviour, and I realise now I need to ask for work that extends me more. And if you could also teach me some techniques for self-regulating my impulses that would be helpful too.

It is unrealistic to expect students to have an instantaneous epiphany about their behaviour in response to this kind of question. In fact, hostage negotiators, for example, are taught to avoid 'why' because it is 'accusatory' (Voss, 2016, p. 153).

However, asking why a student behaved the way they did is the right question – it is just aimed at the wrong person. This is a question that teachers should answer themselves.

This is not always easy. In the midst of a hectic lesson sometimes all we have time for is to deal with a student's off-task behaviour quickly and pivot back to teaching. However, this can mean that we only address the *symptoms* of that behaviour and not its *cause*. Once the lesson is done, it is worth considering what is driving this behaviour. The best way to do this is to ask a simple question: what is the *function* of this student's behaviour?

Typically, behaviour has a purpose: it helps you get or avoid something. Off-task student behaviour is no different. Whether consciously or unconsciously, student behaviour that is repeated has a function. Understanding what these functions are can give you insights into how to address patterns of behaviour from particular students that you otherwise might find hard to deal with or predict.

> Whether consciously or unconsciously, student behaviour that is repeated has a function.

What are the basic functions of behaviour? For the purposes of this book, we are going to group behaviour into five basic functions:

- attention seeking (to get attention or a reaction)
- stimulus seeking (to engage or entertain themselves)
- avoidance (to evade a particular task or situation)
- acquisition (to get something they desire or access an experience)
- asserting authority (to demonstrate their power or autonomy).

Let's look at each of these functions in a little more detail.

ATTENTION SEEKING

Whether it is the attention of you the teacher or one of their fellow students, a good deal of off-task behaviour is driven by students wanting to be noticed. It is usually easy to bring to mind examples of this 'look at me' behaviour: the student who repeatedly interrupts learning by calling out to their friends or the one who makes an elaborate play of coming in late every morning in the loudest possible fashion.

As a classroom observer, I sometimes witness an interesting variation of this where a student will do something furtively as though they don't want to be caught but repeat what they were doing a second time in a more overt way when the teacher fails to spot them. This is instructive: many students deliberately seek out negative attention from their teacher or their classmates (Cooper et al., 2020). Attention seeking doesn't after all necessarily mean seeking *approval* – sometimes it can be seeking a *reaction*. Understanding attention seeking as an attempt to connect with others, whether negatively or positively, will help you more readily recognise the function of these behaviours.

STIMULUS SEEKING

Not every school lesson or class activity is compelling. Many off-task behaviours are driven by students attempting to make their experience of the classroom more interesting. At its simplest this might be a student rocking back and forth when they are sitting on the mat or humming a song to themselves as they write an essay – behaviours to make themselves feel good. In young children a good deal of stimulus-seeking behaviour is sensory: leaning against a wall to feel its solidity when they should be standing straight in line or wandering across the room in the midst of a lesson to examine the interesting texture of the television's speaker.

However, *stimulus seeking* as defined here is wider than just these kinds of sensory behaviours. These behaviours can run the gamut from a student reading a book when they should be listening or starting the work instead of waiting for instruction through to calling out answers when it is someone else's turn or jumping on tables and screaming out unintelligible noises. The defining feature of stimulus-seeking behaviour is that it is not aimed at an audience but rather it feels pleasing to the student themselves. Indeed, much of the behaviour that is initially labelled attention seeking is, on further review, actually an attempt by the student to keep themselves entertained or engaged.

Understanding that the function of some behaviour is to seek out stimulus gives you a new lens through which to view the actions of your students. The power of this lens is demonstrated by the fact that so many of the teachers I work with get better at predicting the actions of their students – particularly those students who struggle with self-regulation – once they are aware of this function of behaviour.

AVOIDANCE

Many examples of off-task student behaviour occur because the student is trying to evade a task or escape a situation that makes them feel uncomfortable. This might include everything from low-level delaying tactics from a student who finds an exercise challenging through to one who angrily storms out of class because the social demands of group work make them feel very vulnerable. These avoidance behaviours are commonplace (if I ever use the phrase role-play activity in a teaching workshop, you can almost guarantee at least one participant will head out for a toilet break) but sometimes hard to spot. Taking the time to recognise where they are driving your student's actions can help you diagnose the cause of many disparate or seemingly unrelated off-task behaviours.

ACQUISITION

Sometimes students act out because they are trying to obtain something. This might be a tangible object like a ball they want to play with or a tablet they want to use. Alternatively, it might be that they are trying to secure a chance to take part in a preferred activity such as a learning game they enjoy or an opportunity to work outside. Often the link between the student's desire and the actions they are taking to secure their goal (loudly lobbying, grabbing something without permission and so on) are fairly self-evident. However, the frequency, persistency and sheer energy young people bring to securing their goals can be overwhelming. This is why labelling this type of often obvious behaviour is nonetheless important: it help us concentrate our efforts on developing specific strategies for addressing them.

ASSERTING AUTHORITY

In any classroom situation there will be individual students who seek power or who are eager to demonstrate their autonomy. This is understandable: young people are constantly negotiating school rules and the expectations of adults while trying to develop an independent sense of themselves in the world. However, sometimes in trying to establish this personal authority, students clash with their teachers or impinge on the rights of their classmates. This behaviour can manifest in lots of tricky-to-deal-with ways, such as the young person who will always do the opposite of what they are instructed or the student who tries to be dominant in every social interaction. Recognising that these behaviours are driven by the student's need to exercise power or demand a greater say in their own learning can go a long way to helping you deal with them effectively and with greater patience.

A note on functional behaviour analysis:

Functional behaviour analysis (FBA) – the formal process for identifying the motivations behind off-task behaviour – identifies the first four basic functions of off-task behaviour mentioned here but does not recognise this fifth function. Proponents of FBA would argue that asserting authority is not so much a function of behaviour as a means to achieve one of the other functions (Iovanonne et al., 2013). Students might, for example, seek out power to get *attention* from their peers or use it to *avoid* a task they find challenging.

This is argument is persuasive. However, I have found that when working with teachers who are new to teaching or who don't have a training in FBA, it is often useful to include asserting authority as a distinct function of behaviour. Power-seeking behaviours are usually easy to recognise, even for those not used to looking for these behaviours. Iovanonne et al. (2013) suggest that identifying these behaviours doesn't 'provide any information about how the students' behaviors are related to what is going on around them' and therefore offer 'little guidance' in how to intervene (p. 4). My experience though is that these behaviours often occur when students feel a lack of agency and that there is a fairly clear set of responses for addressing this behaviour: build up the student's sense of autonomy by offering them more opportunities to exercise choice and demonstrate their positive leadership qualities. For more information about autonomy, please see Chapter 10.

Identifying functions of behaviour

It is not always easy to determine what is the precise function of a student's behaviour. Patterns of behaviour, for example, will often have more than one function. I taught a twice-exceptional student (he was an intellectually gifted learner diagnosed with ADHD) who would constantly call out during class discussion. His interjections were often ill-timed and distracting, but what he had to say was also deeply insightful. It was obvious to me that these were stimulus-seeking behaviours. However, as I got to know him better, I realised that calling out was also a strategy he used to mask his stutter. If he yelled out what immediately occurred to him, he didn't have to wait with his hand raised wondering if he would be able to get the words out. Behaviours often serve multiple functions like this.

How then do we determine accurately what is driving problem behaviour? In my coaching work I use the antecedent–behaviour–consequence (ABC) model.

ABC MODEL

The ABC model is a quick analytic tool that you can use to identify what triggers off-task behaviours and what immediately follows this behaviour that might be sustaining it. I usually do this on a four-column chart.

Date/time of incident	Antecedent	Behaviour	Consequence

When one of your students has been exhibiting lots of off-task behaviour, use this tool to record the date, the behaviour, the antecedents and the consequences.

Date and time of incident and a description of the behaviour

Dealing with sustained off-task behaviour can be overwhelming, but noting each incident and when it happens helps you see the underlying *pattern* of this behaviour. This might take a few lessons. Some teachers find this process too slow, but you should remember that dealing with entrenched behaviour takes time and that the investment of effort here might actually save you time dealing with this behaviour in the long run.

Antecedents

This involves recording what happened immediately *before* you encountered the off-task behaviour. Noting down antecedents helps you spot the trigger points that are cueing this behaviour. What's often striking is that doing this helps you identify trigger points that you otherwise might have missed: the low-level comment from a peer, a subtle rearrangement in the layout of the room, skipping past the student's hand raised when they were eager to contribute.

I use the ABC process sometimes for analysing positive behaviours. Noting down antecedents has been a powerful way to identify small changes of practice that have a large positive impact on individual student behaviours (Pearsall, 2020).

Consequences

Note down here what happened immediately after this behaviour. This is the part of the process that will help you see more clearly the function of this student's behaviour. What was the student trying to get out of this behaviour? What were they trying to avoid? The antecedent–behaviour–consequence approach has two distinct advantages:

1. **An ABC chart moves you from just describing what happened to thinking about why it happened.** This is important. Some off-task behaviours are so intense that we end up dwelling on the *form* of the behaviour when exploring its *function* will help most inform you how to change this behaviour. I coached a teacher, for example, who was dealing with some very aggressive and threatening behaviour from one of his students. He was able to describe in precise detail these behaviours and even do an uncanny impression of the student confronting him. What he couldn't do was tell me why these behaviours were happening. An ABC chart helped him see these extreme behaviours in the context of the wider lesson (the student was actually the victim of very subtle but pervasive bullying) and he was able put in place strategies that helped both the student and the rest of the class feel much safer.

2. **The ABC analysis process can also help give you a sense of agency.** This is especially important when the behaviour you are monitoring from a student is very challenging. Instead of having to *endure* this student's behaviour you are *analysing* it. This gives you some emotional distance from the situation and a clear pathway of action in what might otherwise be a wearying and frustrating situation. I have used this form of analysis in my own teaching and found that it brought about a powerful switch of mindset. For instance, I taught a student early in my career who was prone to protracted meltdowns that completely

disrupted the rest of the class. My emotional response whenever this happened was to feel a sense of dread. ('Here we go again.') Tracking these meltdowns with an ABC chart helped change this reaction.

I started to see things through an investigatory frame. The minute the behaviours started I would be asking myself questions: What kicked this off? What is this student after? Where is this headed? This made it easier to cope with this situation and, in the long run, stop it occurring.

Once you've recorded this data, take some time to analyse it. You might do this on your own, but I have always found it useful to do this with a partner. Bouncing ideas off each other seems to make it easier to generate a hypothesis about the function behind the student's behaviour. Typically, you write out this hypothesis in the form of the following statement:

When _____ occurs, _____ (student) does _____ in order to _____.

The one trap to be mindful of here is confusing correlation (things that occur together) with causation (where those elements actually have a cause-and-effect relationship). The meltdowns mentioned in my earlier example, for instance, tended to occur when the student worked in small teams, but that was not what was causing the behaviour. The simplest way to ensure you don't fall into this trap is, once you have generated your theory, test it. Go back to your class and see whether similar events and environment generate similar behaviour. If they don't, reconsider your hypothesis. If they do, you can start thinking about what you can do to modify the situations that are generating these behaviours.

Conclusion

It may be that in the busy day-to-day of your teaching this process is too time-intensive for all but the most serious cases of off-task behaviour. However, the principles behind functional behaviour analysis can inform your everyday teaching. Many teachers I work with find that once they have used this approach for a specific student, they are more likely to view all off-task behaviour with a keener awareness of what precedes and follows it and to devote more energy to working out what drives students to do what they do.

I know that, for me, learning to identify the function of a student's behaviour was a really important step for improving how I dealt with entrenched poor behaviour. Instead of asking my students to explain their actions and then getting them to do the going-through-the-motions step of assuring me it wouldn't happen again, learning about the functions of behaviour put the onus on me to better understand why these behaviours occurred in the first place. Of course, this didn't mean that I could instantly fix these them, but it did mean I got better at discerning what the real issue was and using my limited time to target the core of these issues. Try using these strategies and see if it does the same for you.

Chapter 8
Tailoring interventions for individual student needs

> 'Yeah, but how does that apply to kids with ADHD? I have three of them in one class!'

I am often asked by teachers how can they modify their approach for students with specific learning characteristics: How do I keep students with ADHD on track? How do you use the restorative approach with someone who has oppositional defiance disorder?

These are hard queries to answer.

There is a real danger that in looking at that student through this lens might actually be typecasting them – obscuring their individual needs with a broad label. Your student 'doesn't need your label or second-hand strategy,' Paul Dix (2017, p. 156) bluntly observes. 'You are not dealing with symptoms that need treating. You are teaching a child that needs to be educated' (Dix, 2017, p. 156).

> There is a real danger that in looking at that student through the lens of their 'condition', we might actually be typecasting them – obscuring their individual needs with a broad label.

It doesn't take much to fall into this sort of reductive thinking about students. When you are having a quick debrief about a challenging lesson, it understandable you might use a shorthand descriptor ('David – ADHD') instead of fully essaying the complex cluster of that individual's needs and challenges. Or summarise a classroom incident as being the product of an underlying pattern of behaviour ('Lee is being oppositionally defiant again') rather than discussing all the other contributing factors. The danger, however, is that this shorthand might calcify into your 'take' on the student. It is crucial that when we think about an individual student's behaviour that we do so with as much sensitivity and nuance as possible.

There is a tension here though because *understanding common patterns of student experience* might actually help inform our view of the individuals we teach. There are a large number of social, emotional and behavioural characteristics that can adversely affect a student's classroom conduct. Understanding *how these characteristics are sometimes clustered* might help you develop more sensitive and targeted responses to that student.

How do we resolve this tension? The short answer is that we use research on learning characteristics and educational challenges to *test* and *extend* our thinking. When your standard approaches aren't working with a student, consider whether a different frame of reference might help you modify your approach. Explore the student's behaviour through this lens.

Start by reading the research. Organisations such as the Teacher Learning Network and McREL International regularly publish online summaries of the latest findings on particular educational issues and the best evidence-based practice in our field. Seek out professional learning from qualified experts. Find out who in your school is knowledgeable on the issue or has a record of successfully working with students displaying the same behaviours. Your goal here is not to make an unqualified diagnosis or to seek out one-size-fits-all advice ('All students with ADHD need clear step-by-step instructions') but rather ideas that will prompt your own reflections:

- Does this information help you better understand your student's behaviour?
- Can you use it to anticipate likely problems or defuse potential conflicts?
- Does it offer you ways to better differentiate your lessons for this student?
- Will it help you support the student to take a more active role in the class?

Your answers here should point towards some next steps you can take to support this student.

If you have a student with a diagnosed learning difficulty, look to the professional advice that comes with that diagnosis – and the body of research behind it – as a way to evaluate and modify your approach.

If you are coming to the limits of your practice with a particular student, use the research on learning differences to identify blind spots in your approach and check whether you have developed the technique to support students of all abilities – not just those who are neurotypical and physically able.

If you are noticing that there are certain clusters of behaviour that you struggle to deal with, see if these behaviours are commonly associated with any particular types of learners or educational issues. Research to see if there are also common strategic responses to these challenges. (Remember you are not trying to diagnose students here but rather build your own capacity.)

Once you have reviewed your practice through a new lens, go back to the behaviour analysis discussed in Chapter 7 and look again at what is driving this student's behaviour at this particular moment in the classroom. Your exploration of learning characteristics and behavioural challenges will give you some general principles to guide your work, and the functional behaviour analysis guidance on how you might apply the learning to this specific student.

Let's look at a scenario (based on lived experiences) to explore how this process might work in practice.

You teach a student who on several occasions has fled your classroom after a loud emotional outburst. Recently the student has been diagnosed as austisic. This gives you an opportunity to look into the research around autism to see if it can help you better support this student.

Even a cursory glance at this research would tell you that austisic students may have *meltdowns* and *bolt* in response to feeling overwhelmed (Goldin et al., 2013). In this light, fleeing the room is not an act of disobedience or the student being temperamental – it is a logical response to a highly stressful situation.

You read one interesting article that explains that these overwhelmed responses are sometimes caused by the sensory sensitivities common to many autistic students. You seek out an aide who works with some of the other autistic students in the school, who lists examples of things that have overwhelmed her charges: loud noises, flickering lights, strong smells, classrooms with echoey acoustics and whiteboards cluttered with too much visual detail.

Could sensory sensitivities be driving your student's behavioural issues?

Your year-level team conducts an ABC analysis of the student's behaviour over a period of a fortnight. While there are no meltdowns during this period, you do see signs of distress on a number of occasions. All of these take place during lessons where the noise volume of the class is high. One loud and echoey classroom – an open learning space – seems to be particularly stressful for the student. On reflection, you note that it is this space that the student has fled during past meltdowns in your class.

Your hypothesis then is that it is a sensitivity to noise that is driving the student's behaviour. You test this hypothesis by putting in place a series of concrete interventions: monitoring the classroom noise more closely, arranging a room change where possible and ordering noise cancelling headphones for the student to use when needed.

Remember it is this testing that is crucial to the process. There may be other sensory cues that are actually upsetting the student. Moreover, there are a large number of other reasons why an autistic student might act out in this way: frustration at being unable to articulate their needs or understand instruction, sudden changes in routine and social anxieties are all potential sources of stress, as are poorly scaffolded or differentiated tasks.

Testing some strategies based on this hypothesis will help you see whether sensory sensitivity is the issue or whether you might need to look into other common sources of stress for autistic students.

Finally, review your progress to see if your approach has helped better understand and support this student.

Conclusion

Christine Gibbs is a teacher-leader and an expert on autisim whose work is emblematic of this sort of tailored approach. She uses the broad body of evidence on the challenges that autistic students face to inform and educate teachers on how to better support those students. She is known to echo the words of Dr Stephen Shore, an autism advocate who is on the spectrum, who explains 'If you've met one person with autism, you've met one person with autism.' (Flannery and Wisner-Carlson, 2020). Keep this in mind when you are differentiating your interventions: know as much as you can about the *types* of challenges your students face but target your response to meet *their* precise points of need.

This can take a lot of time and patience, but it is vital if we are to support those who are often the most vulnerable students in our classroom.

Part 3
AVOIDING OFF-TASK BEHAVIOUR

Chapter 9
Transitions and procedures

When I am invited to schools to talk about stopping off-task behaviour before it begins, I usually don't start by talking about students at all, I talk about athletes. Olympic relay runners can tell us a lot about the value of routines in our classrooms.

At the 2016 Olympics, the Japanese men's 100 metre relay team won the silver medal. What was astonishing about this performance was that, based on the average past performance of their runners, the team should have finished seventh. How did they achieve this incredible improvement?

Realising that they could not compete on speed alone, the team coach, Shunji Karube, spent an enormous amount of time drilling his team on an often-overlooked aspect of the race: the baton exchange. When Karube trained his team to alter their handgrip and baton passing technique, the team was able to complete its baton exchanges more than a second faster than its main rivals. This is a massive gain in an event where just 1.14 seconds separated the first and last official finishes in the 2016 final. (Tellingly, two teams were disqualified for actually dropping their batons.)

I mention this story whenever I talk in schools about the topic of this chapter because paying extra attention to a sometimes-overlooked procedural aspect of their practice is precisely what I'm advocating for teachers to do. Transitions and other classroom procedures are often flashpoints for off-task behaviour. For instance, when I review lessons that have gone badly – both those of teachers I coach or my own – I am often able to trace the problem back to a specific moment either at the start of the lesson or when students are pivoting between activities. Similarly, I often observe lessons derail as teachers are handing back work or conducting some other logistical activity.

However, many teachers have not received specific training on how to prevent these problems occurring. Nor have they necessarily been provided with models for how to efficiently execute these procedures and shifts between activities. How do we avoid the potential disruptions here and make our routines quick and seamless?

Everyday classroom routines like transitions and procedures vary depending on the student age group, subject you are teaching and the space in which you are working, but there are some key principles you can apply in most contexts to meet this goal.

Identify inflection points

Look at the patterns of activity in your classroom. These might be established routines such as a greeting ritual or a well-thought-out convention about how you check student work. However, it might just be the default way you ask your students to move between tasks or solicit their attention. Either way, the goal here is to start becoming more conscious about these routine elements of your everyday practice. Here are some prompt questions to help you identify these patterns:

- Do you have routines for getting your students' attention and issuing instructions?
- Do you have conventions about how students ask, discuss and answer questions?
- Do you have classroom procedures for moving students between tasks and organising them in groups?
- Do you have routines for opening and closing your lessons?
- Do you have well-established expectations about how students take notes, organise their work and respond to feedback?
- Do you have routine procedures for how you hand out and take up materials?

When answering these questions, pay particular attention to those routines that always seem to take longer than they should or where students are most likely to become distracted. Refining your class routines will help in most situations, but it is easiest to start where there is most room for improvement. If your students take an interminable amount of time to get into groups or if a specific class procedure is a flashpoint for off-task behaviour, work at this first. Once these issues have been addressed you can move on to making successful class procedures even more efficient.

Describe your routine

Once you have identified what routine you want to refine, think through what precisely you want students to do. This is important because students often fail to complete classroom procedures correctly, not for lack of effort or poor intent but because they don't completely understand what is expected of them. I often observe students – particularly young students – getting confused and distracted when they are transitioning between activities or completing the first part of a procedure but failing to satisfactorily finish it.

> Students often fail to complete classroom procedures correctly, not for lack of effort or poor intent but because they don't completely understand what is expected of them.

They key to avoiding this trap is *chunking*. That is, breaking the procedure into small, clear steps. The behavioural strategies in the first chapters of this book, for example, break the skill of managing off-task behaviour into a series of sub-skills.

Chunking makes it easier for students to know what is required of them, particularly if the procedure is new to the class or requires them to follow detailed instructions (Brown et al., 2014). Read the following excerpt of a teacher preparing her students for a jigsaw task:

There are three steps to the first part of a jigsaw activity:

1. Get into your green groups. The green groups list is on the board.
2. Decide what topic each group member will research.
3. Once everyone has been assigned a topic, I will ask you to move into your research groups. Each workstation is labelled with a topic so you will know where to go.

Teachers will sometimes baulk at using an activity like a jigsaw because they are worried that it might disrupt the class, but breaking what the students have to do into a series of discrete steps that you can walk them through one at a time mitigates this concern.

It is not just your students who benefit from chunking – this approach helps you too. It is easier to implement a new activity if you are following a series of well-defined steps. It is easier to master a new teaching skill if you break it into its constituent parts and learn them one at a time (Lemov et al., 2012). Isolating sub-skills helps skill acquisition for all learners.

Rehearse and review

Once you have established exactly what is required in a classroom procedure, you need to both practise these procedures and give students feedback on how well they are completing them.

A good way to do this for younger children is to ask them to rehearse a routine. That is, rather than asking them to complete a routine as part of an activity, make the procedure the activity itself:

> *Okay, we are going to play a game called* bunching *where we get into different size groups like pairs or groups of four. The goal is to do this as quickly and quietly as you can. Are you ready?*

Moving onto the mat, getting equipment from their tubs and forming small groups are good examples of activities where rehearsal can radically improve the quality of your students' transitions.

Some teachers baulk at this approach. Either they think their students will be too old for this or they feel like they don't have the time to devote to non-instructional issues. This is understandable. If you feel like your students are too mature for this approach or you just don't have time for rehearsal, focus instead on giving student feedback as they complete a routine. Remember that rehearsal might actually save you instructional time as students complete everyday procedures with enhanced efficiency. I once coached a Year 2 teacher who was able to get his entire class, in an orderly fashion, to gather around a table at the front of his room in under twenty seconds. He told me that this took a good deal of rehearsal time to set up in Term 1. However, watching how quickly and quietly he could get his class to gather round him while demonstrated a worked example in maths – and contrasting this with the other Year 2 classes in his team – it was obvious that this investment of time was paying off.

Giving your students feedback on how well they complete a routine or transition is another highly effective way to refine your classroom procedures. This is often an overlooked teaching opportunity, especially with older students. When you are trying to get a class underway or wanting students to transition between activities, it is understandable if you skip over reviewing how quickly they made a transition or responded to a rallying call, but it is worth the time and effort if you want them to do it even better the next time.

This might take the form of *narrating* – using on-task praise to acknowledge what some students are doing well and nudge others back on track:

I can see Tiana has started. Lin and Ben are underway. Tracey is ready.

Or it might be at the end of the session you review what happened and highlight what to keep doing and avoid next time:

We cleaned up the workspace really well. Everyone used their checklists, and all the tools are away. Now we've got the routine down, let's see if we can do it in under five minutes next time.

Tracking student progress against the clock works well whether you are giving feedback during a procedure or afterwards. Students seem to appreciate having a concrete goal to measure performance against, and 'trying to beat our record' gives an energising boost to mundane tasks for students of all ages. Just remember that if you are going conduct procedures against the clock, you might also have to emphasise the importance of completing the procedure well and not just quickly.

The big four routines for transitions and procedures

I am often asked by teachers which classroom routines are most important for maintaining positive classroom behaviour. This is not easy to answer as this depends a great deal on the class. I stand by my earlier advice: if you want to know where to start, the easiest place to begin is the routine where your students are struggling the most. However, regardless of what the most pressing issue is for you, there are four key routines that I think every teacher should eventually aim to master: greeting rituals, do now tasks, rallying calls and transitions.

GREETING RITUALS

Greeting students as they enter your classroom is a great habit to build into your classroom routine. It allows you to make a quick connection with each student, note anyone who seems out of sorts or unsettled and quickly establish standards of behaviour. These things matter. Let's look at each of them.

Making connection

Saying hello to a student, offering an affirming smile or enquiring about their day is a powerful way to build your relationship with them. As we have discussed, the golden rule of teaching is relationship first, task second. Taking a moment to connect before you have to deliver instructions and direct behaviour helps you signal that all personal relationships matter to you. Indeed, for those students who have a lot of trouble regulating their own behaviour, this interaction at the start of the lesson, might be the only moment when you aren't correcting or directing them, so establishing a warm tone is particularly important.

> Taking a moment to connect before you have to deliver instructions and direct behaviour helps you signal that all personal relationships matter to you.

Identifying mood

Greeting students at the door helps you assess how your students' mood might shape the lesson. You can spot students who seem emotionally fragile or disengaged and might be in need of extra support. Similarly, you can identify students who are having trouble with self-regulation and be ready to deal with them in a proactive manner. Greeting students at the door also helps you get a quick read of the whole class. If they are tired or are unsettled from a previous class or something that has happened out in the yard, you can see this and modify your teaching accordingly.

Establishing standards

The strategy of greeting students at the door gives you an opportunity to remind them of your expectations about classroom behaviour. Greeting students is sometimes referred to as a *threshold strategy* because you are signalling that appropriate behaviour is a condition of entry for your class. If a student isn't conducting themselves in an orderly fashion, you check them at the door and ask them to modify their behaviour or even send them to the back of the line to try again. 'Classroom culture is not static from day to day. It is shaped by the opening minutes of a lesson ... whether you intentionally engineer them or not', so taking the time insist on your standards will make the rest of the lesson easier to manage (Lemov, 2015, pp. 356–357).

DO NOW TASKS

You do not always have the time or opportunity to greet every student at the door. Many high school teachers, for example, find that they are the last person to arrive at the classroom, and asking the class to wait outside for them is not always possible or desirable. Others have classes where their students routinely arrive in class in dribs and drabs over a protracted period. In situations like these ones – or if you just want a less teacher-intensive way to start a class – you might try a *do now* strategy.

A do now is where you set up an introductory task for students that they can do without your close supervision. Typically, this is a quick exercise that is written on the board or listed on a worksheet. When students enter the room, they seek out the do now instruction and begin work without you telling them what to do.

A do now is such an effective routine because it frees you up from policing students as they settle, giving you an opportunity to establish other routines. I find that I have time to do things like check in with a struggling student or recap something with a student who was absent – or even just complete mundane tasks such as taking up work or correcting the roll without interruption.

You need to be aware of some potential traps with this strategy:

- Sometimes teachers will set a task that is too large in scope or simply let the activity go on too long – remember that this is an introductory activity, and you want to be able to quickly transition into the lesson proper. I set myself a time limit of five minutes when conducting a do now and strictly adhere to this limit.
- Keep in mind too that while these activities should prompt students to work independently, it is easy to find yourself monitoring the task more

than you should. If you find yourself constantly prompting students about what to do next, revisit the task itself and make sure that it is designed well for independent learning – and once it is, reiterate to students that this is a task they can do on their own.

- You will also need to be watchful that your students don't come to see the tune-in activity as being divorced from their main learning. You need to avoid busy work tasks and irrelevant warm up activities. I often see silent reading used as behaviour management tool to settle the class, but the reading bears little relevance to the topic being learned or even the subject being studied. This is a missed opportunity. Where possible, use the do now to set up the core learning of the lesson. For example, I often ask students to rewrite the learning and success criteria in their own words to help them clarify what is expected of them. Asking students to outline prior knowledge on a topic also works well, as does getting them to complete a reflection exercise on a previous lesson that is linked to the current one.

RALLYING CALL

A *rallying call* is a pre-arranged signal for getting your students' undivided attention. This might be something as simple as raising your hand or as involved as an elaborate call and response routine. In my last book, I devoted an entire chapter to the surveying of these options and discussing the subtleties of rallying calls (Pearsall, 2020). However, if you are just starting out, there are some key principles to master before you look into the nuances of this technique.

Use a variety of techniques

There are dozens of different approaches you can use to get student attention. Non-verbal signals such as hand gestures, whistles or alarms work well, especially in large learning spaces or noisy environments. Call and response routines ('From three', 'Swish' and, 'Hands on top', 'Everybody stop!') are engaging. Countdowns ('3 . . . 2 . . . 1 Eyes this way') are a forgiving rallying call that gives students time to finish what they were doing or just realise that the teacher has called for their attention.

However, if you overuse a single rally call, students will often pay it scant attention. Experienced teachers know that even a highly effective rallying call can become less effective over time. You don't want students only going through the motions of responding to your rallying call, so employ a variety of calls to keep your rallying call routine attention grabbing. Some teachers change their call twice a term – five or so weeks being long enough to embed good habits without the routine becoming stale. Alternatively, I like to use a counter call where every fourth or fifth time I call for my students' attention, I use a different call to keep students on their toes.

> You don't want students only going through the motions of responding to your rallying call, so employ a variety of calls to keep your rallying call routine attention grabbing.

'Badge' rallying calls as being for older students

Sometimes students – particularly young adolescents – are reluctant to have an active role in a rallying call routine. Typically, this is because they see it as being the preserve of younger kids and baulk at the perceived social risk of taking part too enthusiastically. This is based on a misconception: 'rallying calls are often used in the adult world: judges use gavels, NBA referees use whistles, and large committees are called to order' (Pearsall, 2020, p. 52). Rather than explaining this, I tend to just introduce each rallying call as one that is used with older children:

> If I need your attention Year 9, I am going to use a routine I do with my Year 12s.

> Okay Year 4, I think you are old enough now to use a rallying call that I normally only use with high school students.

In my experience, this simple adjustment is often enough to address this social unease around rallying calls.

Aim for economy

Establishing a rallying call can be teacher intensive, so once you have an established routine, try delivering the call in an increasingly minimalist fashion. Progressively drop your volume and make your gestures smaller; you will discover that you can have the same degree of effect but with a much smaller footprint in their interaction. This both increases your authority – you are doing more with less – and trains students to self-regulate their behaviour. Over time this approach will help you shape class interaction in a subtle, low-key fashion.

TRANSITIONS

Moving between activities is a flashpoint for many off-task behaviours. Having a clear, carefully orchestrated transition routine is a good way to avoid this trap. The key here is getting the sequencing of your instructions right. For instance, teachers sometimes make the mistake of telling students who they will be working with before outlining what the task requires, and students don't even hear the task explanation as they clamour to secure their teammates.

The following scaffolded transitions (adapted from Bennet & Smilanich, 1994) lay out a careful sequence of steps and sub-steps for making your transitions as smooth and seamless as possible:

1. Use a rallying call
   - Demand attention using the routine you have established in your class.
2. When, what and who?
   - Nominate *when* students are going to move.
   - State *what* it is they are about to do as part of the next exercise.
   - Explain *who* they are about to begin working with in the next activity. Do not allow the group to move yet.
3. Move now
   - Give the students the *move now* signal.
4. Monitor and review
   - Monitor the transition using teacher proximity – seek out potential off-task behaviour and stand in the immediate vicinity of off-task students to ensure a quick transition.
   - Give specific and positively framed feedback about successful transition behaviour.

This routine takes a bit of practice to become a habit, but it will soon be second nature to you and your students.

Conclusion

The enormous gains made by the Japanese 100 metre relay team suggest that all the other teams should have been as conscious of their baton changes as Shunji Karube's team was. However, this is the paradox of procedures: the steps involved are small enough that you can easily change them but because they are so small and routine they are often overlooked. It is easy underestimate the power of small, incremental change.

The obvious way to address this blind spot is to look at the accumulated effect of all those incremental changes. I often ask teachers to record the amount of time that transitions take from a single lesson. This number is often relatively low but multiplied out by lessons in a day, days in the week and teaching weeks in a year, the number can represent a large amount of lost instructional time. After tweaking the routine to shave a few seconds here and there, we repeat the calculation – and the resultant gains are huge ...

Keep this in mind when you trial some of the strategies explored in this chapter. Even making your routines a tiny bit more efficient can make your classes run a lot more smoothly over the course of a year.

Chapter 10
Establishing student engagement

The best way to manage challenging behaviour is to not have to deal with it in the first place. The difference between the behaviour of engaged students and those that are disengaged is profound. Indeed, throughout this book, the term most commonly used to describe poor student behaviour is simply *off task*. When learning piques student interest and curiosity is driving behaviour, teachers have little need for so-called classroom management techniques. It follows then that ramping up engagement should be one of your primary ways to respond to off-task behaviour.

Obviously, this is easier said than done. Teachers, after all, don't plan to disengage students. However, understanding what engagement is, surveying what research tells us about how to generate it and exploring emblematic examples of engaging classroom activities can give you a picture of how you might modify your teaching to make it as compelling as possible.

This work is divided across the next two chapters. In this chapter we will discuss some broadbrush ideas about what drives student motivation and explore practical examples of how you might put these ideas into action. Chapter 11 echoes this approach, looking at some specific aspects of teaching practice that you can use to further enhance engagement and giving concrete advice on how to apply them in your everyday classroom.

So, what do we actually mean when we talk about student engagement?

Defining engagement

Sometimes I work in schools where engagement is used as a synonym for entertainment. However, fostering engagement requires you to do more than just make classes more pleasurable. Playing a video to the class or opening the lesson with a fun learning game might be diverting, but these activities do not necessarily help students become more connected to their classmates or more involved in their learning. It is important then to have a clear picture of what we mean when we talk about engagement. The technical definition of engagement might sound a little jargon-y: 'a condition of emotional, social and intellectual readiness to learn characterised by curiosity, participation and the drive to learn more' (Abla & Fraumeni, 2019, p. 2). But I like it because it covers how students feel, how connected they are to their school life and how involved they are in the work they are doing. All of these connections – behavioural, emotional and cognitive – are crucial to motivating students. In fact, research suggests that making these connections is as important to 'student success as teacher quality' (Goodwin & Hubbell, 2013, p. 66).

> Fostering engagement requires you to do more than just make classes more pleasurable.

What does this look like in practice?

Fostering engagement

If you feel your students are not engaged – or if they are loudly telling you that they aren't – there are three key drivers of motivation that are worth considering: challenge, choice and purpose. Is the level of challenge in the work appropriate? Are students being offered enough autonomy? Do students have a clear sense of the purpose of their learning? Understanding how each of these shapes engagement is an important first step in creating and delivering more engaging lessons.

Code work problem:

Take a moment to attempt this task.

The cluster of symbols below is a coded message. Can you break this code? There is no key, but I will give you one clue – the message is a letter from me to you:

We will check your answer in a moment ...

BE CHALLENGING

Code work problem:

Take a moment to attempt this task.

The cluster of symbols below is a coded message. Can you break this code? There is no key, but I will give you one clue – the message is a letter from me to you:

We will check your answer in a moment ...

You need to make sure your lessons are carefully targeted at the precise point of your students' needs. It is obviously boring for students to have to sit through an entire lesson about something that they have already mastered. Or experience a lesson aimed so far above their heads that it is irrelevant to them. What you need to be mindful of here is the idea of mastery.

Mastery is the desire to improve, to get that little bit better at a particular skill. It is mastery that drives the student to try the same trick shot over and over again at lunchtime on the basketball courts. It is mastery that makes a student try to finish that level 'one more time' on their gaming console when they should be doing their homework. Mastery is one of the most powerful motivators of human behaviour (Pink, 2009).

Sometimes we can overlook this aspect of engagement. I was once talking to a school leader about a group of students who were very difficult to manage at his school. He pointed them out in the yard; they were standing in a tight circle watching one member of the group throw an apple at the bin. He was uneasy about my suggestion that we needed to make their classwork more challenging. ('Do you really think trying to get better will motivate these guys?') At that moment, the student who threw the apple walked over to the bin and picked it up – his shot had missed – and instead of putting straight back in the bin, he walked back to the spot of his first attempt and tried it again. The principal and I both laughed.

When a class is behaving badly and struggling to stay focused on even the simplest task, it can feel counterintuitive to ask students to do more challenging work. Similarly, when a student is being rude and aggressive towards you, it is sometimes hard to see that their response isn't really about you but a product of their struggle with a task beyond their abilities. Reviewing your students' needs makes it more likely that you will avoid this trap.

There are three key approaches you can use here: task reviewing, addressing mindset and naturalising struggle.

Task review

Whenever a student – or an entire class group – is off task, I ask myself a simple question: is the work *just right* for them?

> Whenever a student – or an entire class group – is off task, I ask myself a simple question: is the work *just right* for them?

Pitching work at your students' precise point of need is hard and requires constant calibration. By routinely checking and modifying what students are expected to do, you can find that Goldilocks point where the work is neither too easy nor too hard. You do not have to do this on your own. Put the question to your students too. For example, I know a successful high school maths program where students are offered different levels and types of work in each lesson and then asked to pick the work that is just right for them. The success of this program has shown the power of training your student to ask this question of themselves too (Parsons & Reilly 2012; Reilly et al., 2009).

Address mindset

Students find it hard to be motivated by a focus on mastery if they think that ability is fixed. If you believe that your ability to complete a task is innate, you require early and easy success or you might drift off task. Perhaps you might give up altogether (Dweck, 1999). Whereas, if a student believes that they can get incrementally better at something, they are more likely to stay on task – even in the face of setbacks (Dweck, 2017).

You should take the time to explicitly teach your students about these fixed and growth mindsets. As I write this, my youngest son is completing a Mindset Mondays homework task his Year 5 teacher set him. He has to come up with five alternative ways to respond to difficult work instead of saying that it is too hard. When you think a fixed mindset is driving off-task behaviour, remind the student of these discussions. (When my son jokingly rephrased the sentence above as 'I don't get this task' I responded with 'I don't get this task *yet* …')

Naturalise struggle

Many students switch into off-task behaviour at the exact moment they should redouble their efforts. There is a large difference between work that is too hard for students to do and that which requires just a bit more sustained effort. All learning requires some struggle. Indeed, many neuroscientists argue that 'moderate levels of stress can actually improve learning' (Horvath, 2019, p. 240). You want to teach students to anticipate that they will encounter some difficulty and that this is a natural part of learning.

Many primary schools use the concept of the *learning pit* to do this (Nottingham, 2017). This pit is the visual analogy for the period of initial struggle or cognitive hard work you have to go through before you master a skill or reach an understanding of a new piece of knowledge. Approaches like this give students a framework for understanding that the difficulties they encounter are a routine phase of learning, encouraging them to show persistence and not let these moments lead to distracted behaviour.

Sometimes, I devote a lesson to specifically highlighting one or more of these strategies. This works well. Start by picking a task that is right on the edge of your students' capacity. Introduce it to your class, letting them know that it will be difficult and that they need to both be mindful of their mindset and show persistence in the face of the inevitable challenges that they will face. Setting effort rather than performance goals can be helpful here. Effort goals focus not on whether you were successful but how dogged were you in attempting to meet your goals. (A performance goal for a footballer might be to successfully make ten tackles whereas an effort goal might be to *attempt* fifteen tackles.)

As you conduct the class, keep up a running commentary reminding students about the importance of demonstrating grit and a growth mindset:

> *Let's rephrase that Darren, as you can't do it yet.*
>
> *Good work, Mandy. She's already up to her third attempt at this.*

At the end of the lesson, debrief with students about their experience: Did they struggle initially? Did focusing on their mindset help them? Did having an effort goal increase their persistence? Were they able to be more successful than they expected?

Think about your own experience of the exercise too: Did having a difficult task actually ramp up engagement? Is there room to set more challenging tasks for this group? Or for specific students?

This deliberate focus on how students deal with challenge is illuminating. Think back to the code word task at the start of this section. Some of you would have skipped over the activity. This might have been about 'cutting to the chase', but for others it might have been about mindset. ('I am not good at code words.') A large number of you who attempted the task would have initially found it difficult. Did you find yourself in the learning pit? ('This is too hard.') However, with persistence, many of you would have been able to solve most or all of the code word. If this exercise had of taken place in my classroom, I would be able to use this as an opportunity to assess how you deal with challenging tasks and use this information to modify the level of challenge in the lessons. This a powerful way to shape engagement and ultimately behaviour. (See the Appendix for more details about setting up your own code word task.)

OFFER CHOICE

The urge to control our own lives is powerful. Offering your students the chance to feel in control of their learning is a great way to foster engagement.

As we have already discussed (see 'Directed choice' in Chapter 6) a young person's experience of the world is heavily proscribed by the authority of all the adults in their lives. Providing students with more choices within their studies is often a welcome contrast to this experience.

> The urge to control our own lives is powerful. Offering your students the chance to feel in control of their learning is a great way to foster engagement.

Offering more choices to our students is not always easy to do. I have coached a number of teachers who struggle with this – at least initially. It was not that these teachers were resistant to the idea of offering more choice; they just couldn't see where this could be done. Curriculums are set. Classroom schedules are tight. Assessment is compulsory. Students can't just cherrypick what they want to learn. Recognising where you can build choice into your everyday practice is, therefore, the key to offering more choice.

The best way to do this is use a framework for spotting these opportunities. I use Carol Ann Tomlinson's work on differentiation to do this (Tomlinson 2014, 2017). Tomlinson identifies four main areas where we modify learning: content, process, product and learning environment. We can offer students more choice in each of these areas.

Content

Giving students the chance to pick the work that they find most stimulating is a simple way to drive engagement. Consider what you are teaching and think about changes you could make to encourage students to take more ownership of what they are doing:

- Could the student choose a topic that reflects their personal interests?

  Find an invertebrate that you are interested in and summarise the information in that chapter.

- Could students choose work according to their abilities?

  Pick the reading that is just right for you.

You can give your students choice about not only what they learn but also *how they get access* to what they learn.

- Could students choose what medium they use to access the content?

  The material on indices is summarised on the PowerPoint, or you could listen to my screencast on adding squared numbers.

- Could students decide how long they devote to exploring the content?

  You can decide whether you want to quickly re-read the poem and start the essay task or join the close reading group with me where will unpack the poem in detail.

Offering choice might include everything from building a couple of options into a worksheet to getting students to pick the topic they are studying in an inquiry learning project. Whatever you option you use, offering more choice about what it is students have to learn encourages them to devote the maximum attention and effort to their work.

Process

Offering choice in the process gives students the chance to decide how they make sense of the content. When you introduce new skills and knowledge to students, they need opportunities to internalise what they have learned. Tomlinson (2001) calls the exercises you use to do this sense-making activities. Offering students some flexibility with how they go about these sense-making activities can go a long way to fostering engagement. When I am thinking about offering more choices around process, I ask the following questions:

- Could I give the class choice about who they do it with?

  You can work on this on your own or with a study buddy.

- Could students pick the complexity of the task?

  Now you can either apply this rule to the questions on proper fractions or, if you are feeling confident, to improper fractions.

- Do students require more or less scaffolding?

  Clive, do you want to use the TEEL sheet to structure your essay, or do you have a different structure you want to use?

- Do students have a personal preference for how they make sense of content?

  Okay, pick how you summarise information best and make a quick summary of the chapter on representative democracy.

Offering students an opportunity to decide how to process new knowledge and skills encourages them to take ownership of what they are learning.

Product

You can also build choice into how students demonstrate what they are learning.

It is easy for what is considered an acceptable learning product to be become narrowly defined. We have, after all, school- and system-level expectations shaping what form assessment takes. However, there are often more opportunities for differentiation than teachers recognise. (Even in final year exams students can apply to have tasks modified to address special needs.)

Tomlinson and Imbeau (2010) suggest that we should think of products as 'authentic assessments' (p. 15). As long as the product meets the learning standards in your school or system, there are myriad ways for students to show you the extent of their skills and understanding:

- You can offer students the chance to vary the form of the task.

  Do you want to do it as an instant picture book or as an essay?

- You can let them choose the audience for their work.

  At whom do you want to aim this piece of writing, Lee? Your peers? Younger students?

- You can give them choices about work timelines or the length of their response.

  Does it suit you to have an interim submission date for the humanities project?

- You can even modify what success criteria – depending on their ability – individual students need to meet to demonstrate they have met their learning goals.

  If that seems too hard at the moment, what would be a sign of success for you? Being able to add improper fractions?

Giving students these kinds of choices about the product will help students feel more in control of and connected to their learning.

Learning environment and culture

Finally, you can offer students some flexibility about the learning environment and how they interact with the people within it. How students feel in their classroom can have a profound effect on their readiness to engage. Designing the learning space and its culture to better meet these individual student needs is a powerful form of differentiation. This is easier when you let their choices guide you:

- Where appropriate you might let a student choose where to sit.

  Find a quiet spot where you think you won't be distracted.

- Give them a chance to decide with whom they might work well.

  Can you pick a partner who helps you do your best?

- Give students the opportunity to move around the room if they struggle to sit in the one spot for protracted periods of time.

  You can decide when you need to get up and stretch your legs – just make sure you don't interrupt others.

In my experience, offering students options like these will give them a greater sense of agency in the classroom and make them more likely to actively engage with their learning.

When choice is not an option

Of course, there are situations where students can't really be offered opportunities to demonstrate autonomy. You might be able to find ways to modify aspects of your curriculum, but you can still run into the limitations of the students themselves. In many instances, the age or ability of those you are teaching makes it impossible for them to make informed choices. It is often better, therefore, for 'teachers to make an executive decision on behalf of their pupils, and then work to boost *buy-in* for this choice' (McCrea, 2020, p. 97).

So, how can we boost buy-in?

Give them clear, concrete explanations for your decisions:

> *Reviewing your timetables will make it easier to complete the work on simplifying fractions.*
>
> *Once you have learned the basic TEEL structure you will be able to use it to write paragraphs in all your essay-based subjects.*

This helps your students understand the benefits of what you want them to learn. Learning demands effort, and helping them see why this effort is worth it will increase buy-in. (For a more extensive discussion of how having clear aims increases motivation, see the next section 'Establish purpose'.)

You can also bolster buy-in by giving students the opportunity to actively opt in to your decisions. Peps McCrea (2020) suggests that this might be as simple as preceding the task with a micro-choice ('Shall we have a go at this?') or by conducting more involved exercises such as asking them to summarise how the learning might help them address a personal need or signing a learning contract.

The key here – whichever strategy you use – is that if you can't give your students choice, see if they can better understand and support your choices.

ESTABLISH PURPOSE

We are much more likely to be engaged if we are working towards something worthwhile. Our students need to feel like what they are doing matters. It is not enough for the purpose of learning to be implicit – we need to explicitly tell students how what they are learning links to a bigger purpose.

> Our students need to feel like what they are doing matters. It is not enough for the purpose of learning to be implicit – we need to explicitly tell students how what they are learning links to a bigger purpose.

Students need to know at the lesson level how the *activity* they are doing links with their *learning*. This is not always apparent for students. In my book *Fast and effective assessment* (2018), I talk about how, as a classroom observer, I used to ask students what they are learning in a given lesson, and they would often to reply by telling me what they are doing. ('I'm learning the Age of Exploration handout.')

In recent years, there has been a real push in Australia at both the school and the system level to address this issue. A very high number of the schools I have worked with have put time into establishing learning intentions and success criteria as mandatory elements of instruction.

A *learning intention* is a statement that makes explicit what learning – not just what activity – students will focus on in that lesson or group of lessons. Typically, learning intentions are written in a simple and direct fashion:

We are learning to write topic sentences.

This does not mean that you are expected to avoid novel ideas or new terminology – note here that *topic sentence* has a particular meaning in literacy and English classes – but rather that specialist vocabulary and challenging ideas are couched in clear and concise sentences. This ensures students understand the core purpose of the lesson.

A good way to test whether your learning intention is really focused in this way is to ask yourself if it focuses on skills or knowledge that could be used *beyond* the lesson. For example, this intention is lesson specific:

> *We are learning today to apply gouache to our self-portraits.*

Whereas something like this more explicitly refers to a skill that students might use in other lessons:

> *We are learning to apply gouache to a canvas.*

Effective learning intentions also tend to be paired with success criteria. *Success criteria* are benchmarks by which students can judge whether or not they have successfully met the learning intention. Ideally, these should be differentiated so that students of all abilities know what they have to do to achieve success.

Again, success criteria are written in simple, clear language – often in the form of *I can* statements:

> *I can identify topic sentences in an essay.*
>
> *I can introduce the key idea of a paragraph in a single sentence.*

Or you may wish to frame these as questions:

> *Do I know the difference between gouache and watercolour?*
>
> *Did I create a colour wheel before I put paint to canvas?*

Either way, the test here is whether or not students can use these statements to know what success should like and then use them as a compass point to guide them towards that goal.

Obviously, just because you tell students the purpose of what they are doing doesn't mean that they engage with this goal. Therefore, it is important to take a moment to get students to demonstrate their understanding of learning purpose to help them embed it in their thinking. There are several ways you might do this:

- offering students three success criteria but letting them offer suggestions for a fourth
- asking students to highlight words in the learning intention that they aren't familiar with or don't understand
- getting students to rank success criteria from what they think will be the easiest to achieve through to the hardest
- requiring students to rewrite the learning intention in their own words
- showing students the task and asking them to predict what the success criteria will be and then comparing predictions with actual criteria
- providing students with an inverted model that depicts precisely what not to do in their answer and ask students to identify the weak points in this response
- matching exemplar responses to teacher comments to show how teachers rank work against a set of standards
- providing students with a patchwork rubric and asking them to fill in the blank section of the rubric, judging what is required for that criterion or level of achievement (Pearsall, 2020).

Your students don't just need to have a sense of purpose at the lesson level for them to really engage – they need to have it at the unit or subject level too. Effective learners can link what they are doing to a wider body of knowledge. You need to help your students see how what they are doing draws on their prior knowledge and connects to their bigger goals.

If my students are failing to make these connections – despite my best efforts to weave this into the lesson – I will use a dedicated activity to remind them. The *connect, extend, challenge* (CEC) protocol is emblematic of this style of activity (Project Zero, 2015). In it you ask students to list the following:

Connect	How is what you are learning connected to what you already knew?
Extend	What new ideas did you get that extended your thinking in new ways?
Challenge	What is still challenging or confusing about what you are learning? What questions and wonderings do you still have?

Alternatively, ask students to do a quick diagram of how what they have learned in the lesson or unit connects to their wider learning. Both of these activities are effective and easy to use, and students get better at them the more you use them.

What we are trying to do here is a build a narrative about how their learning. Narratives are a powerful force for keeping students on task. There is a tendency among students to see a lesson in isolation. (I had a colleague who used to say students treat classes like a free-to-air television: 'What's on today?') Being able to describe how today's lesson links with a wider unit or make a compelling narrative about their learning fits into a bigger story about their own life helps address this tendency.

I once had a teacher in a workshop challenge me about this idea. He felt that he didn't have the time ('Telling stories? I barely have time to cover the curriculum . . .') to remind students of something they should be doing anyway. ('The story is sit in your seat and actually do some work.') However, creating narratives isn't a diversion from the key purpose of the class – it is a reminder of what this purpose is.

This is not an esoteric idea. At the micro level we know that there is hard science to show that we remember details embedded in wider narratives better than as isolated facts (Horvath, 2019). It is easier, for example, to remember twelve random words if you can assemble them into a short narrative.

At the macro level, we know that a strong narrative can shape our broader experiences as learners. We know, as learners ourselves, that it easier to persist with a dry or difficult task if we can see that doing it will help us achieve a larger goal. The same is true for students. This is why making connections to real-world activities is so crucial. Indeed, Abla and Fraumeni (2019) listed making these connections between the curriculum and real-world outcomes as one of the key research-based strategies for engaging students. When students can place an individual task or topic into a bigger story of their own development, they are much more likely to see the activity as meaningful. In Bridgeland et al.'s (2006) survey of former high school students, 81 per cent said they would have found school more engaging if there was more real-world learning and links to future work in their studies. Tellingly, the students surveyed were ones who had dropped out of school.

Of course, links to future work prospects is just one narrative that students can use to frame their learning. It is rather an emblematic example of a wider point: helping students establish why what they are doing matters is an important aspect of creating engaged and on-task learners.

> The key to making these strategies work is scaling success. Look to turn small successes into big ones.

Conclusion

After a tricky class, it is hard to reflect on the degree of challenge built into the activity or if the underlying purpose of the learning was clear. Similarly, it is challenging to have to pause in the midst of a confrontational encounter with a student and ask yourself 'does this student have enough autonomy?'

What makes this particularly difficult is that much of what contemporary research (Wilkinson & Klaes, 2018) tells us about drive and decision-making is counterintuitive (see Chapter 7). When I coach teachers who are really struggling with a class, I will ask them how they are modifying their students' work to ramp up engagement. Often, they will tell me about a detailed series of consequences they have put in place if their students don't remain on task. Sometimes they respond by telling me about an elaborate series of rewards they put in place to motivate their students. This carrots and sticks method is common, but the research suggests that it is, in the long run, actually quite ineffective – in some cases even reducing engagement (Deci et al., 1999; Smith et al., 2015). Focusing on rewards and consequences might be a natural first step but doesn't tend to produce the results that teachers desire; 'they result in short-term changes but in reality they promote compliance and little else' (Smith et al., 2015, p. 6).

Given that intuitive approaches are often ineffective, it is important to reflect on your approach to engagement with both patience and a critical eye. Don't ask yourself, 'Was the whole class engaged?' Instead focus on individual students: 'Were there any students whose behaviour was changed during this activity?' Similarly, if you are trying to engage a particular student, don't make a broad assessment of the whole session – instead take careful note of fluctuations in their attentiveness. Be alert to subtle shifts in dynamic. The key to making these strategies work – as with many strategies for building positive classrooms – is scaling success. Look to turn small successes into big ones. Once you have mastered one strategy, try others.

Of course, this all takes time but not as much time as having to deal with each individual off-task behaviour. You don't go into teaching to police students. It is much more interesting to focus your energies on encouraging students to connect with their learning. This is a sometimes-unspoken truth about making lessons more engaging for students: it makes them more engaging for you too.

Chapter 11
Enhancing student engagement

In the previous chapter, we explored the importance of offering students challenging and meaningful work with built-in opportunities to demonstrate some autonomy as to how they might best explore this learning. These ideas were taken from a body of research that explores the sometimes-counterintuitive forces that drive human motivation and engagement (Kahneman 2011; Wilkinson & Klaes, 2018).

However, there are some other elements of engagement to be mindful of if you want to further enhance your students' connection to their learning. For a start you need to acknowledge that when focusing on challenge, choice and purpose, these forces will be less effective if you have a combative and fractious relationship with your class. Relationships matter – being able to connect well with your students will maximise the approaches outlined in the previous chapter.

You also need to be mindful about what recent developments in neuroscience can tell us about engagement. While you need to be wary of overstated claims about research into the brain, understanding some key insights from the science of learning and cognition about what garners our attention will help you enhance what is compelling about your lessons.

Similarly, measuring the impact of these strategies and those covered in the previous chapter, will help you refine your approach to student engagement. Whether your lessons are engaging should not be something you simply intuit from student behaviour – actively seeking out feedback means you have a responsive and proactive approach to making your classes as compelling as possible.

Let's look at each of these aspects of engagement in detail.

Build relationships

Having a strong relationship with a student means that you are much better at calibrating your teaching to their needs. By getting to 'know your students you will be able to judge when to push your students and when to back off' (Wiliam & Leahy, 2015, p. 108). You can better recognise when they are struggling and see opportunities for when they might be extended. However, good relationships do more than allow teachers to assess and refine student engagement – in many instances they determine whether students engage at all.

You can most readily see how much relationships matter when you give your students feedback. One of the main determinants of whether or not someone acts on a piece of feedback – the literature on feedback often labels these *triggers* – is their relationship to the persons who gives this feedback (Stone & Heen, 2014). Students will readily accept even critical feedback if they trust you. However, it is just as easy for a lack of trust to undermine that feedback. Whenever you deliver feedback, the 'contents of comments' invariably gets mixed with 'your feelings about the giver (or about how, when, or where she delivered the comments)' (Heen & Stone, 2014, para. 15).

It was once suggested to me by a colleague that if your feedback was good enough, it shouldn't matter who gives it. Perhaps that *should* be the case, but we know it *does* matter. The real issue for me though is not whether relationships influence how students learn but what we do to improve and maintain good relationships. The next section will explore some strategies that I have found effective.

TOUCH BASE FREQUENTLY

Trust is built on repeated interactions. Think about how ambivalent feelings about a co-worker soften once you got to know them better. Or the way disparate extended families grow closer with shared experience. The social physicist Alex Pentland (2014) argues that 'the amount of direct interaction between two people predicts ... the shared level of trust' between them (p. 70). Even more importantly, the number of direct interactions is a very precise measure of 'the strength of social pressure exerted between people' (Pentland, 2014, p. 70).

Perhaps you suspect that, to some degree, this work confuses cause and correlation. Don't we, after all, interact more with people we trust? However,

Pentland's research clearly echoes the anecdotal experience of many teachers: if you want to have more influence with your students, you need to check in with them frequently. Greeting students as you come into class, catching them behaving when they are working well and asking about their welfare on a routine basis are ways to build up this connection. Sometimes when you have a fractious relationship with a student, the temptation is to interact with them less. Clearly, the answer is actually to connect more.

> Sometimes when you have a fractious relationship with a student, the temptation is to interact with them less. Clearly, the answer is actually to connect more.

MAKE PERSONAL CONNECTIONS

If you want to build a relationship, you have to get to know the whole child. What are their interests outside of your classroom? What aspects of their life beyond school shape their behaviour in school? It is not enough to check in frequently about a student's work; you want to take the time to enquire about them too. Of course, this doesn't mean becoming immersed in the minutiae of their private lives but rather looking for quick opportunities (see Chapter 9) to show that you are interested in them not simply as a student but as a person.

This also works the other way: your students need to see you as a person too. This takes some finesse. Teaching involves developing a professional persona. A persona requires you 'to be yourself. But be yourself on a good day' (Goodwin & Hubbell, 2013, p. 87). You may need to be more serious in class than you are with your workmates or more rigorous about deadlines than you are in your personal life. Having a persona maximises your impact but gives you some professional distance too. You do not have to abandon this distance – do not reveal private details about yourself.

Giving students a sense of your personal interests can help build your relationship with them. A well-chosen anecdote or references to your own experiences as a learner can go a long way to helping students make a personal connection to you and your teaching.

There is a big pay-off in building relationships in this way: 'teachers who make even a modest effort to develop personal connections with students … significantly increase those students' academic motivation' (Martin & Collie, 2016, p. 8).

HAVE FUN

You want your students to know that while learning can be hard work, it is also enjoyable. Make sure curiosity and play are part of your curriculum. Learning games are student favourites. Use them to raise the energy level of class when interest is flagging or to lighten the mood when conflict has undermined your connection with particular students. I particularly like to use learning games to rehearse foundational knowledge and investigate new concepts. *Whiteboard relay* and *race the bell* (see Appendix) are both examples of learning activities that generate thinking but also give you an opportunity to see students in a new light.

Of course, having fun means demonstrating your enthusiasm for learning too. An enthusiastic demeanour makes you much more approachable to students. As does having a sense of humour. Sometimes teachers take this advice to mean they have to be funny. This is not the case. There is clear evidence that humour ramps up student engagement, but in terms of building relationships, results are more mixed (Banas et al., 2011). I sometimes encounter, for example, teachers whose take on 'having a sense of humour' is being sarcastic or using jokey put-downs. This approach might hold students' attention ('The class was laughing') but clearly in the long run damages relationships. ('Yes, but was the student?')

The approach here is not about being funny so much as it is bringing a lightness of touch to your teaching: treat your own failures as learning opportunities with a self-deprecating sense of humour. If it suits the situation, try using some levity to defuse potential conflict. Set high expectations for student achievement but insist on these standards in a warm, positive tone. This warmth of tone will make it easier to connect with students and also make your classroom a more pleasant place for you to work.

A final note on building relationships to drive engagement: anticipate failure. At first, all the work you are putting may have no effect. The research about relationships is that a person's view of you is fixed – until it isn't (Cone et al., 2017). When a person changes their mind about you, there is usually a precipitating event that gives them a strong emotional reaction. This event seems to abruptly change their mind: 'impressions don't gradually melt like candlewax ... they flip on a dime' (Horvath, 2019, p. 207). However, all the attempts you make to connect to a student make this sudden change more possible and indeed more likely. Anticipate that it will take some time to build a better relationship with a student – that it might take many attempts to trigger an emotional turnaround – but be reassured that when you finally see the payoff for all your hard work it happens very quickly. Remember, too, that positive relationships have a compounding effect. Humans are social creatures whose actions are often shaped by those around them (Service et al., 2014). Therefore, the more positive relationships you have in a class, the more likely *all* students are to engage with learning.

> Set high expectations for student achievement but insist on these standards in a warm, positive tone.

Pique curiosity

One of the biggest developments in the last twenty years of teaching is our growing understanding of how the brain works. We now have a much better sense of how memory functions, what types of practice are effective for skill development and the kinds of strategies that are most helpful for retaining information in the long term (Brown et al., 2014).

This understanding of the brain is partial. You should be sceptical of programs making grand claims about simple exercises ('brain training', 'listening to Mozart') that will transform students' learning (Goodacre, 2008). However, the new science of learning has highlighted the importance of how we use variation to engage our students.

VARIATION

The brain prefers to remember than to think. It is easier, after all, to recall information that you already know than have to expend energy learning something new. In response to the demands of learning, the brain – where possible – 'seeks patterns, shortcuts, and quick, generalized solutions that require less conscious thinking time' (Pearsall, 2020, p. 7).

As a result, learning can become routine. Generally, this is helpful. When faced with new knowledge or skills you can fall back on familiar study habits and strategies as a safe base from which to learn. Teachers draw on this all the time. Having established classroom routines means you spend less time giving instruction and monitoring behaviour (see Chapter 9); presenting work in a uniform way means students can concentrate on the content instead of you having to explain the format of each individual piece of information. Routines help us 'make the most of our ability to think less about the things we repeatedly do' (McCrea, 2020, p. 60).

However, there is a trap here. Sometimes these cognitive shortcuts lead to students thinking less: going through the motions instead of working hard, giving familiar tasks only cursory attention, and responding to challenging questions with pat responses.

This is where variation comes in. A change of pace or a novel approach can re-engage student attention and re-energise the class. There are three key reasons why this is the case: variation is attention grabbing, variation is moderately stressful, and variation is memorable.

> A change of pace or a novel approach can re-engage student attention and re-energise the class.

Variation is attention grabbing

Changes of pattern stand out to the brain. This is true within individual learning activities and across learning sequences. At the micro level, this is easiest to see in how students process visual information on worksheets and lecture notes. If one element of visual information you present to students differs from all the others – what neuroscientists call a *singleton* – then it is more likely to engage your attention (Theeuwes, 1992). Moreover, singletons (for example, a bolded due date on a homework sheet, a single new slide layout in a lecture) are more likely to stay fixed in your memory (Rajsic et al., 2016).

At the macro level, the arresting nature of novelty can be seen in lots of other aspects of a learning sequence. Switching up the type of activity students are doing or the way you deliver information is a useful strategy to garner more attention: the content covered in the class taken outside or the skill taught in the learning game that breaks up the lesson stand out to students because they represent a break in the regular pattern of learning.

Moreover, it helps make your own experience of teaching more engaging. Indeed, there is some research to suggest that recurrent novelty in the workplace has long-term cognitive benefits (Oltmanns et al., 2017).

Variation is moderately stressful

As teachers we are aware that high-stress environments – a student's difficult home life, a noisy or fractious classroom – can inhibit learning. Low-stress environments can inhibit learning too. Students are less likely to engage and remember work that is repetitive or boring or delivered in a formulaic way. Indeed, experts on boredom believe that it is a sort of 'compass that helps us to avoid squandering valuable resources on environments and strategies that are no longer likely to yield a worthwhile return on the investment' (Goldberg & McWelling, 2018, p. 20). What students need then is an element of struggle – what are sometimes called moderate stressors – to engage their thinking. Variation is the kind of moderate stressor you can build into your everyday learning to maximise engagement.

> Students are less likely to engage and remember work that is repetitive or boring or delivered in a formulaic way.

This can take all kinds of forms: breaking up the lesson into a series of short discrete tasks, punctuating classes with the kinds of novel learning activities shown in the Appendix, or using a wide variety of strategies to deliver and assess learning. To demonstrate the power of using variation, play two games of noughts and crosses with a colleague. Play the first game with traditional rules, but in the second game, compete against your partner to see who can lose the game. This simple change radically changes the level of engagement any participant gives this familiar activity. Demonstrating this in a workshop of teachers, I often point out that teachers are quieter when they play the second time and how many of them had brows furrowed with concentration during the game. After the activity, though, they are often louder and more engaged as a group. This increase in concentration and energy is typical of how varying tasks can heighten engagement (see 'Inverted models' in the Appendix for how you might apply this idea in your classroom).

Variation is memorable

Many teachers I coach believe that the *skill and drill* approach of getting students to do something over and over again – what researchers call *massed practice* – is the most effective way to learn. However, the belief that 'learning is better when you go at it with single minded purpose' is actually a misnomer (Brown et al., 2014, p. 47). Research into the science of learning actually suggests that *spaced* and *interleaved* practice is a more effective approach (Cepeda et al., 2006). What does this entail?

Instead of studying something in a single sustained period, try *spaced practice* where you return to a topic or skill over a longer period of time. Spacing the learning gives your students a better opportunity to consolidate their learning as they process information in a more protracted way and then have to retrieve it multiple times. This leads to longer-lasting learning (Cepeda et al., 2006).

Similarly, using *interleaved* and *varied practice* where you chop and change between different activities and topics – as opposed to focusing on a single activity and topic – helps your class develop a deeper understanding of what they are studying (Carvalho & Goldstone, 2014).

Sometimes the easiest way to foster engagement is to offer students more variety. Anticipating where in your lesson design or course outline learning might seem repetitive or dry and building more variation into the learning in these moments can go a long way to keeping students focused. This is particularly true of students whose stimulus-seeking behaviour (see Chapter 7) sometimes leads them off task.

It is worth noting, though, that the effects are not always immediate. Reformatting a worksheet so that the key information is more eye-catching or breaking up a routine activity with an energetic learning game will generate an observable up-tick in student engagement. However, the effects of other types of variation are more subtle and are effective in the long term. Spaced and interleaved learning are classic examples of this. Students find these types of learning hard work and actually often prefer massed practice (Brown et al., 2014). Keep this in mind when you are designing your courses. Plan your lessons with a variety of activities to maintain your students' immediate attention, but also think about how to use variation over the long term to encourage students to have a deep and sustained engagement with their learning.

It is worth thinking about how contemporary technology aimed at young people makes use of these lessons about variation. Console games, smartphones and social media platforms all use variation to hook and maintain the attention of our students. In many ways these devices and platforms are our direct competitors for student attention, and we should make sure we make the most of these strategies in designing engaging lessons.

Seek feedback

Across this chapter and the previous, I have laid out five strategies for building student engagement: be challenging, offer choice, establish purpose, build relationships and pique curiosity. As we have seen there is a clear body of research that supports these strategies, but it is crucial that you assess whether they are working in your class. After all the question is not whether your students *should* be engaged, but *are* they?

In my experience, a lot of the assessments of student engagement are inferred. This makes sense: it is easy to see when a dry or difficult task leads to students losing interest and veering off task or when an engaging activity generates lots of student engagement and curiosity. However, if you want a richer sense of how engaged a student is, it is best to ask the student themselves.

> If you want a richer sense of how engaged a student is, it is best to ask the student themselves.

QUESTIONING

Questioning is an important component of each of the aspects of engagement we have explored. Questioning allows you better understand students and to pitch work at the precise point that will challenge them (Pearsall, 2018). It gives you a mechanism for teasing out your students' interests and prompting their curiosity (Caram & Davis, 2005). It provides you with more clarity around their learning goals and more choices about how they might go about meeting them.

Sometimes overlooked, though, is that questioning can be a tool for keeping up an ongoing sense of how well your students are engaged (Hattie, 2009). I encounter many schools that place real emphasis on regularly checking in on student performance but far fewer where questioning focuses explicitly on engagement. Avoid this mistake. Questioning is a great way to encourage engagement (Abla & Fraumeni, 2019), but it is also an effective way to *assess* engagement.

The key here – as with all questioning – is to focus on learning as a dialogue (Hattie & Zierer, 2017). Keep checking in with students, letting them know that whether they are engaged and to what degree is part of the ongoing dialogue that you have with them about their learning.

Obviously, you don't want this to conversation about engagement to devolve into students just disparaging a lesson if they don't find it fun or thinking that they can opt out of a task because it doesn't hold their interest. Nor do we want students to simply tell you whether a class is boring or not. We want a genuine dialogue about the degree of their engagement and the reasons that are shaping this reaction. This requires some careful application of questioning technique. I have written extensively elsewhere (Pearsall, 2018; Pearsall, 2020) about the best techniques for starting a dialogue with your students that apply in this situation, but there are some things you need to be particularly mindful of when you are talking about engagement.

Wait time and turn and talk time

If you are asking the whole class for feedback, you want to hear from as many students as possible. When teachers are exposed to whole-group data for the first time (see 'Measuring engagement' on page 112), they are often surprised that their impressions of student engagement are incorrect; they have let a vocal minority shape their views. Don't let a handful of voices dominate the feedback.

Use *extended wait time* to avoid this trap. Ask about student engagement and then wait at least three seconds before you seek out answers. This will increase the quantity and quality of responses you get from students (Pearsall, 2020). Asking students to turn and talk to a partner for forty-five seconds or so before you seek out responses is a particularly effective way to embed this extended wait time. Your students' responses will be more considered and – as they are reporting on a conversation rather than just their personal opinion – they tend to feel less vulnerable when giving their feedback.

Golden questions and model answers

You also need to encourage students to offer justifications for their thinking. One of the ways to do this is to follow up your student's initial response by explicitly asking them the *golden question*: What makes you say that? The golden question is a versatile, low-key way to remind students of your expectations about explaining their opinion. Indeed, sometimes students unconsciously internalise these expectations so that they will include the question in their response when you haven't even used it:

> *I think it could have been more accurate, and what makes me say that is ...*

Another effective way to do this is to model the kind of explanation you are seeking. I sometimes tell students that their response will need to contain a *because* or list on the board a range of reasons ('It wasn't clear why we are doing this', 'We got to choose our topic') that they might draw on when answering why they may – or may not – have been engaged by the task.

Pause time and elaboration cues

You can also encourage students to elaborate in more subtle ways. Extending your pause time – the duration you wait after an answer before you respond – is a highly effective way to elicit more details and clarification from your students. As we have discussed (see 'Restorative chat' in Chapter 5, page 53), conversational turn taking often kicks in during the briefest gaps in conversation. This is often exacerbated in classrooms where teachers are under constant time pressure to 'get through' the content and students get used to the teacher immediately evaluating their response.

Not cutting in at the end of a student's initial comment, then, is a powerful signal to them that you want them to elaborate further on their response. If it feels unnatural not to say anything at this point, you might try offering an elaboration cue. This might consist of a non-committal placeholder statement ('Okay ...', 'Mmm ...') or a quick gesture encouraging the student to continue.

Being mindful of how you use pause time and other elaboration cues is particularly important when you are seeking out feedback one-on-one. This can be an intimidating situation for some students, and it ensures you give the student proper time to articulate their reflections.

Snapshot feedback

Sometimes you don't have time for this type of questioning, so instead your queries take the form of a snapshot question. This is where you do a quick whole survey of your class's level of engagement:

> *Rank how engaged you are by this activity.*
>
> *In one sentence explain to what degree this lesson engaged you.*

This might involve strategies such as a first to five summaries, traffic light rankings or, if you are at the end of the lesson, students submitting their feedback to you as exit passes. This might not offer you much in the way of dialogue, but it certainly provides quick feedback about engagement that you can respond to in subsequent activities or lessons.

Many teachers want to take this one step further and not just ask students about their levels of engagement but actually measure it.

Measuring engagement

Measuring student engagement 'can't *directly* [my emphasis] increase or improve engagement' (Abla & Fraumeni, 2019, p. 4), but having meaningful before and after data can certainly help you target and assess your efforts to improve student engagement. Many schools and school systems do this via attitude to school surveys that are periodically given to students. This is a useful approach and one worth investigating.

However, a lot of this data is taken annually or over the course of a term or semester. If you are working with a challenging class that you want to engage better, this might be the wrong time frame. If this is the case – or if you want some additional individual lesson data – you might try one of the tools described in the next sections.

TIME ON TASK TOOL

This tool requires you to check in at intervals throughout the lesson and indicate on a seating chart which students were on or off task at this check-in point. Popularised by Jim Knight (2017), the time on task tool gives you a sense of the pattern of engagement across the class and throughout the lesson. You can then use this data to map the ebb and flow of engagement during the lesson or contrast and compare different approaches between lessons. I have used the tool as both a teacher and a teacher coach and have found that because the check-in points are mandated by a timer, the tool often helps you see more clearly flat spots in the lesson or pockets of disengagement that you might have otherwise missed.

STUDENT ENGAGEMENT SAMPLING TOOL

One of the common criticisms of the time on task tool is that what constitutes on-task behaviour to a teacher or observer is sometimes unclear. How do we distinguish, for example, between a student who is genuinely engaged with the task and one who is dutifully completing the task but is actually bored and disengaged? The engagement sampling tool addresses these concerns. You use it to periodically poll students as to whether they are non-compliant, compliant or engaged by the activity they are doing (Knight, 2017). This worked well in my class but really took off when I changed the categories to the following:

- green (I'm into it)
- amber (I'm doing it)
- red (I'm over it).

These traffic lights made intuitive sense for my students – they liked the clear difference between being compliant and actually engaged – and it provided useful data for adjusting my teaching. If you trial this approach in your class, make sure you set aside some time to unpack what each category means as this will help improve the accuracy of the tool and encourage students to take an active role in giving you feedback.

The tools and surveys discussed here help you make dispassionate assessments of whether your classes are as engaging as you hope they are. Do not be discouraged if the data says they aren't. It is better to know what is driving off-task behaviour than to always be reacting to symptoms of this disengagement.

Conclusion

You should think of the time you spend on the strategies discussed in this chapter as an investment. Your commitment to everyday relationship-building helps, over time, to create a more connected and conscientious group of students. Your focus on designing lesson plans and asking questions that offer variety and pique curiosity mean you don't have to devote as much energy to addressing the problems that arise when students are disinterested and distracted. Your commitment to ongoing reflection about the extent of your students' engagement ensures that all these efforts will be as targeted and effective as possible.

At times, this might feel like yet another responsibility to add to your workload. But this is the central point of the last section of this book. We do not want to always be countering what students do wrong – we want to concentrate our attentions on helping them learn. Having a nuanced understanding of how to enhance engagement means we can ensure that this learning is deep and lasting. Rather than adding to what we have to do, this focus on enhancing engagement actually ensures that what we do has impact.

Conclusion

Sometimes when you read a student's reports from different teachers, it is like you are reading the reports of completely different students:

____ must learn not to get upset ...

____ is a pleasant and cooperative student.

____ spends too much time avoiding work and talking in class.

____ has completed all set tasks to a high level.

____needs to develop some self-discipline ...

____ is a well-behaved and enthusiastic student.

____ must learn to tolerate activities that he himself may not enjoy.

____ participated well in all classes activities – even leading some ...

This variation of behaviour we see right across age levels from early learning centres to senior school settings. It varies with teacher, task or even just time of day. Observe a primary school student and you will often see their behaviour alter subtly – or not so subtly – as they move back and forth between their regular teacher and the specialists who teach them art or PE. Stand in a high school classroom where the class is staying on but the teachers are changing over and watch as the whole class's behaviour shifts almost instantly as one teacher leaves and the next arrives. I can see this variability in my own experience as a student – every one of the quotes in this conclusion were written by my middle school teachers about me.

This inconsistency can be a real source of frustration for teachers – note the mystified tone of my teacher here:

He is totally enigmatic. He appears to have a completely rational and incisive intellect that grasps abstruse points easily, but he has not submitted any of the assessment tasks this term.

However, it is also an opportunity.

If a student's behaviour is inconsistent, dependent on mood and context, and prone to sudden shifts, then it is also *malleable*. Student behaviour is not fixed. Indeed, one of the biggest mistakes we can make when trying to build a culture of positive and cooperative classroom conduct, is seeing the current behaviour of a particular student or a class as what it will always be. Every activity in this book is built on the premise that all students can – and regularly do – change.

> If a student's behaviour is inconsistent, dependent on mood and context, and prone to sudden shifts, then it also *malleable*.

Of course, this does not mean that the change is always helpful or improvement is automatic. Teaching is often marked by struggle, setbacks and long slogs for small victories. This requires real perseverance. It takes both energy and empathy to turn around a class whose behaviour is difficult or help a student who is making bad decision after bad decision.

The most effective teachers know that the patience and care that they bring to this project can't just be directed at their students – it has to be directed at themselves too. This is a point too easily skipped over when we talk about creating positive classrooms. Teachers are often their own harshest critics. We need to have realistic expectations about what we can achieve and demonstrate genuine self-compassion when assessing our own performance. We can't hold ourselves to standards by which we would never judge a colleague.

As a teacher leader and coach, I have had to challenge teachers on this issue many times. This usually takes the form of simple reflective question: if this was happening to another teacher, what would your advice be? It is remarkable how often recasting the problem in this way is enough for the teacher to start talking about realistic expectations, small steps and being gentle with themselves. Often this advice to a hypothetical colleague is delivered with a wry expression or tone that indicates that the teacher is aware of the double standard to which they have been holding themselves.

Occasionally, though, a teacher will defend this double standard: shouldn't we have, goes their argument, the highest expectations of ourselves?

Absolutely, we should. However, we have to be careful that these expectations don't actually undermine our goals. Teaching is about playing the long game. Creating real and enduring change takes time. We don't want our students to just be compliant – we want them to take ownership of their behaviour and become independent and responsible members of our community. This is hard work. Being unnecessarily critical of ourselves or failing to acknowledge small victories can undermine the sense of agency and momentum we need to meet this goal.

> Teaching is about playing the long game. Creating real and enduring change takes time.

Moreover, we need to be especially mindful of our own resilience. Taking care not to compromise our own wellbeing is not something we do just for ourselves. We need to guard our optimism and energy so we can be the most effective educators and advocates for the young people we teach – and all those who will be in our care in the future.

A few years ago, I returned as a consultant to the high school I went to as a student. Some of the teachers who wrote the reports quoted at the start of this conclusion were still teaching at that school. The first thing that struck me was that it seemed to me that they hadn't really aged. I suppose that to my fifteen-year-old self, anyone over thirty seemed middle-aged ... and now, twenty-five years on, those teachers were in that phase of their life.

What really stood out, though, was that when I had a chance to chat with some of the teachers I respected most as a student, they still seemed to take delight in teaching young people. They were active participants in the workshop (I did notice the odd wry expression when I mentioned a tactic for dealing with able but argumentative students) and spoke warmly afterwards of the students they were currently teaching.

The approach of these accomplished educators is emblematic of what is described in this book:

- You should try to see the best version of who a student might be – even when (especially when) they aren't behaving in that way at the moment.
- Aim to be constantly learning – no matter the stage of your career – refining the strategies that you use to help students realise this best version of themselves.

- Understand that a warm, positive and compassionate approach makes it easier to sustain this effort – particularly when things are challenging.

Hopefully, *Classroom Dynamics* offers you practical and easy-to-adapt techniques that you can use over a long career – or just help you get through a difficult day.

Appendix

BREAK GLASS IN CASE OF EMERGENCY LEARNING GAMES

Line debate

This debating game is a fun way for students to practise giving their own point of view and to help them understand those of others. It is often used as a precursor activity to essay writing but is effective for unpacking any contested issue or hotly debated topic.

HOW DO YOU RUN A LINE DEBATE?

- Nominate the topic students will be debating. You might select an essay prompt or a question that informs the subject of your lesson:

    Macbeth is responsible for his own fate. Discuss.
    The hitch kick is the best long jump technique.

- Divide the class into affirmative and negative teams and have them stand on either side of the room. Make sure you include the whole class – this activity tends to be more engaging when every student is involved in the task and students can't opt out into a spectator role.
- Explain that they are going to have to come up with arguments to support their assigned side of the debate irrespective of their personal views on the topic. This is important as it gives students a layer of protection. They are not offering their own point of view but rather imagining what someone on that side of the debate would argue. You will find that positioning students as 'key informants' in this way makes them much more likely to take academic risks.
- Explain the basic rules to them:
    - Speakers from each team take turns presenting their arguments. Emphasise that you will not be going down the line but rather seeking out volunteers.
    - If the speaker is able to successfully offer an argument that hasn't been presented yet by their side, they select one member of the opposition to join their team. (Make sure you tell the class that once a team member changes sides three times, they are locked and can't change sides again. This ensures that no student feels singled by their classmates.)
    - Once a student changes sides they have to come up with arguments that present the side of the debate that they are now on.

- If no team member can offer an argument, the adjudicator (usually the teacher but sometimes a student umpire) will nominate someone to join the opposition team.
- Gives students an opportunity to brainstorm some potential talking points in small groups and then conduct the debate. Usually, line debates run for ten to fifteen minutes, ending when either all of the arguments have been exhausted. Don't be in a rush to wind up the activity; arguments tend to come in waves and sometimes teams will pass several times before finding a new line of argument and then make a quick comeback. Being prepared to wait for students to volunteer, prompting students ('Can I hear from someone who hasn't spoken yet?') or offering students some extra turn and talk time to brainstorm some more will all help kickstart the debate again.
- Make sure you record the arguments in some fashion. A lot of good class discussion gets erased by the bell, so make sure you either take notes, assign a student scribe or video the debate. This way students can draw on the discussion in their later learning.
- It works well if you end the line debate with a reflection activity. This might take the form of a class discussion or summary writing task. My personal favourite is to complete a continuum activity where they indicate their personal viewpoint by placing themselves across the room on a continuum from strongly agree with the prompt to strongly disagree. You then ask them to justify their placement and watch as other students move back and forth on the continuum based on the student's reasoning.

Continuums are a great precursor activity for line debating – and a good alternative for very young students who might struggle with line debating. I have seen line debating played effectively with students as young as Year 2, but if you have students younger than that you might want to use a continuum as way to introduce students to the concept of mapping opinion through movement.

Line debates incorporate physical movement, playful competition and good-natured argument. I always found them to be a great way to energise my class and a real student favourite. Try line debating in your own class and see if this is the case for you too.

Race the bell

This activity, which is also known as *race the clock* and *beat the buzzer*, is a whole-class review activity where students take turns asking and answering a question on the topic they have been studying. It is a great way to check for prior knowledge when returning to a topic or to review how well students have understood what you have just covered in a lesson.

HOW DO YOU RACE THE BELL?

- Start by asking your students to formulate two or three questions on the topic they have been learning about. The questions can range widely across the topic but remind them that they should be factual questions. (If you want to look at more contested or subjective issues, use a line debating activity instead.) Some students may need some modelling about the types of questions you are after. Indeed, with younger students you may even present students with a list of questions that they can choose from.
- Ask the whole class to stand (or if they are unable to stand, indicate in some other fashion that they are in an 'up' position). Explain the basic game play of race the bell:
    - A student will volunteer to ask a question of the whole class.
    - If someone else can answer that question, both the person who asked the question and the person who answered sit down.
    - If no one answers correctly, the person who asked the question remains standing.
    - The game ends when either everyone is seated, or the alarm or bell rings.
- Start the game. Students are usually eager to get out of class, so there will often be a chorus of responses to easier questions. To ensure an orderly class, insist on getting students to put their hands up and then use this to your advantage by carefully selecting students to who might usually be more reluctant to answer. Students realise quite quickly that to get out in this game you don't have to answer a question, you can just ask one, so you should see students become more at ease as the game wears on.

- Don't accept wrong answers; the playful nature of it being just a game provides students with a layer of protection, so don't hesitate to say if something is incorrect. Just refer the question back to another student to see if someone else might know the answer. (If no one can answer it, make a note of the question on the board for further follow-up.) Do the same with partial or incomplete answers and then let both respondents sit down when the answer has been fleshed out.
- Anticipate that often the bell will ring or the timer will go off before everyone is seated. This is fine: the time limit keeps the class focused and adds to the playful feel of challenge. Even if students don't successfully finish, they will still be energised (notice how many tell other students as they are leaving what they were going to ask), and you will have a better sense of where to target your next lesson.

> Very young students may struggle with this activity: formulating questions is a higher-order skill. As to a lesser extent is selecting the one you want to ask. Even the self-regulation required for the basic game play can be difficult for young students. Therefore, you may want to try instead the up 'n' down game where students are presented with a binary choice (capital or lowercase letters, odd or even numbers) and your students have to indicate their choice by either standing up or sitting down. It also works well if you use it to assess student understanding (true or false, teacher explained it well or should say it again) – especially if you ask students to explain why they answered the way they did.

Race the bell is a versatile and highly engaging activity. It might take your students a couple of tries to catch all the nuances of the rules, but it doesn't take long for them to get the basics. When I survey students about the most popular learning games, it always ranks close to the top, so don't be surprised if it becomes one of your most requested activities.

Inverted models

Inverted modelling is a classic strategy that you can use when, despite trying lots of things, you haven't been able to get students to engage with your advice. It consists of presenting students with an example of precisely what not to do and asking them to spot in what way this model has failed. You can also do this by having students create an inverted model that they then annotate to highlight the flawed nature of a piece of work.

HOW DOES INVERTED MODELLING WORK?

- A word of warning: this approach doesn't suit all students or apply to all situations. It is a strategy you typically use after you have made your expectations clear about what is expected of your students. You don't want the activity to confuse them – you want it to reiterate your message about what success looks like. Nor do you want to 'send signals that anything less than their highest standard of work is acceptable' (Pearsall, 2020, p. 48), so make sure you use inverted models in a calculated and targeted fashion.
- Start by creating a model response that features all of the common errors that you typically see associated with a particular task. This approach works just as well for work products in arts and technology subjects as it does for written work. If you teach subjects where students perform their work such as physical education or drama, you might wish to rehearse the inverted model as a demonstration or even record it as a video.
- You may need to review past student work to get a complete list, but most teachers have a good sense of what a particular class is struggling with or what are the common errors associated with this specific task. If you or the class are new to inverted modelling, start with examples of very poor work – as opposed to those that are just low level – as this will make your message clearer.
- Present the inverted model to the class and ask them to highlight what is unsuccessful about the response. This tends to work well as a small group activity. Your students may need some scaffolding, such as a list of common errors to look out for, to make this task easier. Similarly, if you are asking students to create the inverted model themselves, provide them with samples of bad work or error checklists to use as a

starting point. (This will also help them see that creating a poor work sample is a serious task and not a chance to create something silly or inappropriate.)

- Make sure you reiterate to students that while correcting or creating these extreme examples can be fun, this task has a clear and serious purpose. Follow-up is everything with inverted models. The key is carefully twinning the inverted model task with a follow-up task where students have to apply what they learned to their own work. Asking students to explore what not to do should have reminded them about what they should be doing, but you want to check that is actually the case.

Inverted modelling is enlightening and entertaining and a great back-up activity. Use these models whenever you feel students are falling into poor work practices that you can't shift. They are a terrific way to help students see the underlying purpose of a task and to engage their sense of mastery.

Whiteboard relay

This is a group brainstorming activity where students compete to see which team can produce the most answers under time pressure. Running totals of their efforts are constantly updated during the activity, which leads to concentrated and intense game play. Whiteboard relays are an ideal activity for when you want students to quickly review something you have already taught them or indicate the extent of their prior learning outside of your class. They are also an effective strategy if you want students to come up with a wide range or a high volume of ideas very quickly.

HOW DO YOU ORGANISE A WHITEBOARD RELAY?

- Draw a scoring grid on your board. It should look something like this:

Running total	Group A	Group B	Group C	Group D	Running total
7					7
11					11
17					17
23					23
29					29
30					30
30+					30+

- Divide your class into groups of four to six. Ask the groups to come up with a name. Or if you are concerned that this might take too long (or produce inappropriate suggestions), assign a name for each group.
- Explain the basic game play to the class:
  - They have to brainstorm a specified number of facts and ideas as quickly as possible. One scribe in each team must keep a running total of these facts and ideas as a written list.
  - When they reach one of the benchmark numbers listed in the running total column of the scoring grid, a team member will come up to the front and put a tick in their column next to that number.

- The winner is the first group to a specified number. However, there is room on the scoring grid for them to add to that total as other groups work towards the goal number.
- One real issue with this engagement activity is that sometimes it is *too engaging*, with students getting rowdy as they are swept up in competing against other groups. Anticipate this by setting clear expectations about what is appropriate behaviour during this activity. Emphasise that there will be no running in the classroom (docking points from students' totals works well to enforce this rule) and make sure students know what the rallying call is if you need their attention.
- Do not tell your students what the topic of the brainstorm is until you are ready for the activity to start because once students know, they will want to share their ideas with their team – and any further instructions you have will be upstaged.
- Start the activity by telling students the topic of the brainstorm. Move around the room monitoring the teams' progress, making sure they are updating their running totals.
- If the competition becomes uneven with one group taking an insurmountable lead or others falling so far behind that they might lose interest, there is an elegant way to level the competition. Simply pause the class and ask the teams to take turns reporting back three of their answers – with the only proviso being that they can't report back suggestions that have already been offered. This will help groups who have fallen behind catch up to the other teams but preserve enough of a lead for the top teams that they won't protest too much.
- Once the activity is complete, ask students to share their unique answers and discuss what you have learned as a group. You may want students to complete a reflection activity where they summarise and synthesise this knowledge in some way. My favourite example of this is to ask the teams to group their responses into three or four categories – a higher-order task that gets them thinking about how they might organise the information they have produced.

Whiteboard relays are a highly effective way to turn simple recall tasks into a dynamic classroom activity. You can use them to make a flat spot in a lesson plan livelier or to channel the energy of a group whose enthusiasm is becoming disorderly into a more focused application of effort.

Code word task

This is a classic team-building exercise where a team of students decode a message without the use of a key. While the message itself might be something you want students to dwell on, the real appeal of this exercise is that it helps teach your students the value of persistence and teamwork.

To create the code, write a short letter to your students outlining a key concept or message about something you are studying. Make the message briefer than you would normally for students of this age level. Write it only in lower case, without punctuation and double space the paragraphs. Use a minimum of eighteen-point font. Now convert the message into a nonsense font such as Windings or Webdings.

- Divide the class into small groups and explain that they will be attempting to decode a message. Do not downplay the difficulty of this task – it works better if you foreground what will be challenging about the task:
  - There will be no key to the code.
  - There is no punctuation.
  - Some words will start on one line and go to another.
  - Students will only receive one clue about the code.
- Distribute the code to students face down on their desk. Signal the start of the activity by giving them their one clue: the code word is a letter from me to you. Most groups will quickly realise that this means the letter will open with something like 'Dear students' and end with a formal sign off such as 'Yours sincerely' and your name.
- This should give the groups enough of a hint to decode the whole letter, but monitor groups closely in case you need to offer extra help in the form of a subtle hint or leading questions. Be very careful about intervening too early – the key lesson here is that while at first glance the code is nearly impossible to break, with enough sustained effort all of the groups should be able to crack it without a lot of teacher intervention.
- Move around the groups, giving updates to the class when a group has an important insight or finishes a line or paragraph. This will help keep students focused, but usually you do not have to do much in this regard – after a few minutes students are often engrossed by the task and somewhat oblivious to your presence. The challenge is getting

students' attention again when you want to wind up the activity. To help avoid this problem, give students a few minutes' notice before stopping. If some groups finish early, ask them to summarise the message in exactly twenty-one words to ensure they have read it properly for meaning.

- When you do finish the exercise, use a rallying call to get everyone's attention and ask your students to flip over the sheet so they can't keep doing the code. Once they are listening and have their pens down, ask them to flip it back over and get the winning group to read out the message. You might want to also get students to share or have a go writing themselves a twenty-one-word summary.

- However, don't just debrief about the message, discuss the task itself with your students. Did they find themselves in their learning pit? What strategies worked well to get themselves out of it? Note what you saw too and ask them how they might apply what they experienced when faced with other learning challenges.

Code words are the most popular of all the learning games featured in my books. Many times, I have taught or been observing a class and seen normally unruly students riveted as they compete as a team to crack the code. This activity is the best example I know to remind teachers how engagement can transform student behaviour.

About the author

Glen Pearsall is quite simply Australia's most dynamic and engrossing author and presenter on student engagement in the classroom."

Michael Victory, Teacher Learning Network

Glen Pearsall's reputation is built on his long record of bringing about real and lasting change in student behavior in both Primary and Secondary schools. He is Australia's most acclaimed educational consultant.

Miles Campbell, Teacher Training Australia

Glen was a Teacher Leader at Eltham High School and board member of the Victorian Curriculum Assessment Authority. He works throughout the world as an educational consultant, specialising in engaging instructional practice, student behaviour, feedback and assessment, differentiation, peer coaching and workload reduction for teachers.

Glen has been a Cambridge Education associate, a master class presenter for TTA and a research fellow at the Centre for Youth Research, University of Melbourne. Glen has a long association with the Teacher Learning Network and Critical Agendas and was the founding presenter of the widely popular PD in the Pub series. He is also co-creator of Toon Teach, an animated series on creating positive classrooms.

Glen is the author of the best-selling *And Gladly Teach* (2010), *Classroom Dynamics* (2012), *The Literature Toolbox* (2014), *Fast and Effective Assessment* (2019.) He is the co-author of *Literature for Life* (2005), *Work Right* (2011) and *Tilting Your Teaching* (2020). His ebook on questioning T*he Top Ten Strategic Questions for Teachers* (2013) was translated into Khmer for Cambodian teachers. Glen's latest project has been a collaboration with TTA to create argumentative AI avatars with whom teachers can practice their techniques for pivoting around arguments and de-escalating potential conflicts.

Glen can be contacted at Amba Press or via email at pearsallglen@gmail.

References

Abla, C., & Fraumeni, B. R. (2019). *Student engagement: Evidence-based strategies to boost academic and social-emotional results.* McREL International.

Banas, J. A., Dunbar, N., Rodriguez, D., & Liu, S.-J. (2011). A review of humour in education settings: Four decades of research. *Communication Education, 60*(1), 115–144. https://doi.org/10.1080/03634523.2010.496867

Bartlett, T. (2013, January 30). Power of suggestion. *The Chronicle of Higher Education.* https://www.chronicle.com/article/power-of-suggestion/

Bennet, B., & Smilanich, P. (1994). *Classroom management: A thinking and caring approach.* Bookation.

Bradley, K. K. (2008). *Rudolf Laban.* Routledge.

Bridgeland, J. M., DiIulio, J. J., & Morison, K. B. (2006). *The silent epidemic: Perspectives of high school dropouts.* Civic Enterprises. https://files.eric.ed.gov/fulltext/ED513444.pdf

Brown, P. C., Roediger, H. L., & McDaniel, M. A. (2014). *Make it stick: The science of successful learning.* Belknap Press.

Caram, C. A., & Davis, P. B. (2005). Inviting student engagement with questioning. *Kappa Delta Pi, 42*(1), 18–23.

Carvalho, P. F., & Goldstone, R. L. (2014). Effects of interleaved and blocked study on delayed test of category learning generalization. *Frontiers in Psychology, 5,* Article 936. https://doi.org/10.3389/fpsyg.2014.00936

Cat, S. (2018). *PDA by PDAers: From anxiety to avoidance and masking to meltdowns.* Jessica Kingsley Publishers.

Cepeda, N. J., Pashler, H., Vul, E., Wixted, J. T., & Rohrer, D. (2006). Distributed practice in verbal recall tasks: A review and quantitative synthesis. *Psychological Bulletin, 132*(3), 354–380. https://doi.org/10.1037/0033-2909.132.3.354

Cone, J., Mann, T. C., & Ferguson, M. J. (2017). *Changing our implicit minds: How, when, and why implicit evaluations can be rapidly revised.* In J. M. Olson (Ed.), *Advances in experimental social psychology: Vol. 56. Advances in experimental social psychology* (pp. 131–199). Elsevier Academic Press.

Cooper, J. O., Heron, T. E., & Howard., W. L. (2020). *Applied behaviour analysis* (3rd ed.). P&C Education.

Deci, E. L., Koestner, R., & Ryan, R. M. (1999). The undermining effect is a reality after all—Extrinsic rewards, task interest, and self-determination: Reply to Eisenberger, Pierce, and Cameron (1999) and Lepper, Henderlong, and Gingras (1999). *Psychological Bulletin, 125*(6), 692–700. https://doi.org/10.1037/0033-2909.125.6.692

Dix, P. (2017). *When the adults change, everything changes: Seismic shifts in school behaviour.* Crown House Publishing.

Dweck, C. S. (1999). *Self-theories: Their role in motivation, personality and development.* Psychology Press.

Dweck, C. S. (2017). *Mindset: The new psychology of success* (Updated ed.). Ballantine Books.

Flannery, K.A. and Wisner-Carlson, R. (2020) 'Autism and education', *Child and Adolescent Psychiatric Clinics of North America,* 29(2), pp. 319–343. doi:10.1016/j.chc.2019.12.005.

Fischhoff, B. (1996). *The Real World: What good is it? Organizational Behavior and Human Decision Processes,* 65(3), 232–248. https://doi.org/10.1006/obhd.1996.0024

Gladwell, M. (2009). *What the dog saw: And other adventures.* Little, Brown and Company.

Goldberg, R., & McWelling, T. (2018). Induced boredom suppresses the recall of positively valenced information: A preliminary study. *Psychological Thought,* 11(1), 18–32. https://doi.org/10.5964/psyct.v11i1.249

Goldin, R. L., Matson, J. L., Tureck, K., Cervantes, P. E., & Jang, J. (2013). A comparison of tantrum behavior profiles in children with ASD, ADHD and comorbid ASD and ADHD. *Research in Developmental Disabilities,* 34(9), 2669–2675. https://doi.org/10.1016/j.ridd.2013.04.022

Goodwin, B., & Hubbell., E. R. (2013). *The 12 touchstones of good teaching: A checklist for staying focused every day.* ASCD.

Hattie, J. (2009). *Visible learning: A synthesis of over 800 meta-analyses relating to achievement.* Taylor & Francis.

Hattie, J., & Zierer, K. (2017). *10 mindframes for visible learning: Teaching for success.* Routledge. https://doi.org/10.4324/9781315206387

Heath, C., & Heath, D. (2013). *Decisive: How to make better choices in life and work.* Random House.

Heen, S., & Stone, D. (2014, January–February). Finding the coaching in criticism. *Harvard Business Review.* https://hbr.org/2014/01/find-the-coaching-in-criticism

Herndon, J. (1971). *How to survive in your native land.* Bantam Books.

Horvath, J. C. (2019). *Stop talking, start influencing: 12 insights from brain science to make your message stick.* Exisle Publishing.

Iovanonne, R., Anderson, C. M., & Scott, T. M. (2013). Power and control: Useful functions or explanatory fictions? *Beyond Behaviour,* 22(2), 3–6. https://doi.org/10.1177/107429561302200202

Joyce, B., & Showers, B. (2002). *Student achievement through staff development* (3rd ed.). ASCD.

Kahneman, D. (2011). *Thinking fast and slow.* Farrar, Straus and Giroux.

Kegan, R., & Lahey, L. L. (2002). *How the way we talk can change the way we work: Seven languages for transformation.* Jossey-Bass.

Kerbey, L., & Fricker, E. (2023). *The educator's experience of pathological demand avoidance: An illustrated guide to pathological demand avoidance and learning.* Jessica Kingsley Publishers.

Knight, J. (2017). *The impact cycle: What instructional coaches should do to foster powerful improvements in teaching.* Corwin.

Lemov, D. (2015). *Teach like a champion 2.0: 62 techniques that put students on the path to college.* Wiley.

Lemov, D., Woolway, E., & Yezzi, K. (2012). *Practice perfect: 42 rules for getting better at getting better.* Jossey-Bass.

Lewis, R. (2008). *The developmental management approach to classroom behaviour: Responding to individual needs.* ACER Press.

Mackay, J. (2006). *Coat of many pockets: Managing classroom interactions.* ACER Press.

Mackay, J. (2020). *Creating a positive learning environment: The savvy teacher.* Oxford University Press.

Martin, A. J., & Collie. R. J. (2016). The role of teacher–student relationships in unlocking students' academic potential: Exploring motivation, engagement, resilience, adaptability, goals, and instruction. In K. R. Wentzel & G. Ramani (Eds.), *Handbook of social influences on social-emotional, motivation, and cognitive outcomes in school contexts.* Routledge.

McCrea, P. (2020). *Motivation: Harnessing the science of motivation to boost attention and effort in the classroom.* Author.

Murphy, L. K. (2020). *Declarative language handbook: Using a thoughtful language style to help kids with social learning challenges feel competent, connected, and understood.* Linda K. Murphy.

Murphy, L. K. (2021). *Moving from 'Get' to 'Give' PDF, In Co-regulation Handbook: Creating competent, authentic roles for kids with social learning differences, so we all stay positively connected through the ups and downs of learning.* Linda K. Murphy. https://tinyurl.com/4n9uh2c5

Nottingham, J. (2017). *The learning challenge: How to guide your students through the learning pit.* Corwin.

Oltmanns, J., Godde, B., Winneke, A. H., Richter, G., Niemann, C., Voelcker-Rehage, C., Schömann, K., & Staudinger, U. M. (2017). Don't lose your brain at work – The role of recurrent novelty at work in cognitive and brain aging. *Frontiers in Psychology, 8*(117). https://doi.org/10.3389/fpsyg.2017.00117

Parsons, J., & Reilly, Y. (2012). *Maths in the inclusive classroom.* Teaching Solutions.

Pearsall, G. (2018). *Fast and effective assessment: How to reduce your workload and improve student learning.* ASCD.

Pearsall, G. (with Harris, N.). (2020). *Tilting your teaching: Seven simple shifts that can substantially improve student learning.* McREL International.

Pennebaker, J. W. (2013). *The secret life of pronouns: What our words say about us.* Bloomsbury.

Pentland, A. (2014). *Social physics: How good ideas spread – the lessons from a new science.* Scribe.

Pink, D. H. (2009). *Drive: Surprising truths about what motivates us.* Penguin.

Project Zero, Harvard Graduate School of Education. (2015). *Connect, extend, challenge.* http://www.pz.harvard.edu/sites/default/files/Connect%20Extend%20Challenge_0.pdf

Rajsic, J., Sun, S. Z., Huxtable, L., Pratt, J., & Ferber, S. (2016). Pop-out and pop-in: Visual working memory advantages for unique items. *Psychonomic Bulletin & Review, 23*, 1787–1793. https://doi.org/10.3758/s13423-016-1034-5

Reilly, Y., Parsons, J., & Bortolot, E. (2009). *Reciprocal teaching in mathematics* [Paper presentation]. Of Prime Importance: The 2009 MAV Annual Conference, Bundoora, Vic, Australia.

Rogers, S. L., Howieson, J., & Neame, C. (2018). I understand you feel that way, but I feel this way: The benefits of I-language and communicating perspective during conflict. *PeerJ, 6*, e4831. https://doi.org/10.7717/peerj.4831

Service, O., Hallsworth, M., Halpern, D., Algate, F., Gallagher, R., Nguyen, S., Ruda, S., & Sanders, M. (with Pelenur, M., Gyani, A., Harper, H., Reinhard, J., & Kirkman, E.). (2014). *EAST: Four simple ways to apply behavioural insights*. The Behavioural Insights Team. https://www.bi.team/wp-content/uploads/2015/07/BIT-Publication-EAST_FA_WEB.pdf

Smith, D., Fisher, D., & Frey, N. (2015). *Better than carrots or sticks: Restorative practices for positive classroom management*. ASCD.

Stivers, T., Enfield, N. J., Brown, P., Englert, C., Hayashi, M., Heinemann, T., Hoymann, G., Rossano, F., de Ruiter, J. P., Yoon, K.-E., & Levinson, S. C. (2009). Universals and cultural variation in turn-taking in conversation. *Proceedings of the National Academy of Sciences of the United States of America, 106*(26), 10587–10592. https://doi.org/10.1073/pnas.0903616106

Stone, D., & Heen, S. (2014). *Thanks for the feedback: The science and art of receiving feedback well*. Penguin.

Theeuwes, J. (1992). Perceptual selectivity for color and form. *Perception & Psychophysics, 51*(6), 599–606. https://doi.org/10.3758/BF03211656

Thorsborne, M., & Vinegrad, D. (2009). *Restorative justice pocketbook*. Management Pocketbooks.

Tomlinson, C. A. (2001). *How to differentiate instruction in mixed-ability classrooms*. ASCD.

Tomlinson, C. A. (2014). *The differentiated classroom: Responding to the needs of all learners* (2nd ed.). ASCD.

Tomlinson, C. A. (2017). *How to differentiate instruction in academically diverse classrooms* (3rd ed.). ASCD.

Tomlinson, C. A., & Imbeau, M. B. (2010). *Leading and managing a differentiated classroom*. ASCD.

Truman, C. (2021). *The teacher's introduction to pathological demand avoidance: Essential strategies for the classroom*. Jessica Kingsley Publishers.

Voss, C. (with Tahl, R.). (2016). *Never split the difference: Negotiating as if your life depended on it*. Random House Business.

Wiliam, D., & Leahy, S. (2015). *Embedding formative assessment: Practical techniques for F–12 classrooms*. Hawker Brownlow Education.

Wilkinson, N., & Klaes, M. (2018). *An introduction to behavioural economics* (3rd ed.). Macmillan.

Index

Abla, C, 116, 128, 140, 142
absolute negatives, 43-44
acknowledgement 73-, 75-76
acknowledgement pivot, 57-58, 72
acquisition 88, 90
active listening pivot, 57
agency, 39, 44, 50, 63-64, 91-93, 124
agreement pivot, 52-53, 58
agreement prompts 30-31
anonymous individual reminders, 22
antecedent-behaviour-consequence (ABC) model, 92-93
antecedents, 92-93
appropriate behaviour, 6, 109, 158
attention grabbing, 111, 136-137
attention-seeking behaviour, 18
autism, 97, 99-100
autonomy, 38, 65, 91
avoidance, 88-90

beat the buzzer, 153
begging and bargaining, 29
boredom, 137
brevity, 28
Bridgeland, JM, 128
bullying, 29-30, 93

capability, 47
capacity, 47
Cat, S, 39
carrots and sticks, 129
cause, 88, 94
CEC (connect, extend, challenge) protocol, 127
check ins, 17-19

choice, 42-43, 62-69, 120-125
chunking, 105-106
citing past efforts, 31
class reminders, 20-21
classroom routines, 104, 107, 136
code work task, 116-117
collaboration signals, 62-63, 74
collaborative approach, 41-42
collective progress checks, 17-19
commands
    invisible commands, 23
    micro commands, 28-30
    non-verbal commands, 40, 46, 110
    respectful commands, 27
connect, 127-128
connection, 108, 116, 131, 133-134
consequences, 35, 66, 92-94, 129
considered choice, 81
context 47-48
context check in, 80
control 37-38
cross praise, 15-16
culture, 109, 123-124
curiosity, 135, 139
curriculum, 1, 128

declarative language, 38-40, 48-49
declarative statements 39-50
describing, 14, 34, 81
demands, 2, 38, 47-49
demand-avoidant, 37-47
directed choices, 37, 64-65
Dix, P, 31, 51, 54, 97
do now tasks, 109-110

ECA (empathy, content, action) technique, 33-34
effective approach, 5-7
effort over ability, 13-14
elaboration cues, 141
emotional context, 33
empathy, 33, 57
empty praise, 13
enhancing student engagement, 131-144
entrenched off-task behaviour, 85
environment, 38, 48, 123-125, 137
establishing standards, 108-109
exit point, 27
explicit instructions, 25-36
extended wait time, 46-47, 140-141
external attribution, 55
eye contact, 14, 20, 63

face-saving cues, 68-69
feedback, 23, 60, 106-107, 132, 139-142
Fischhoff, B, 43
foreground choice, 42-43, 62
Fraumeni, BR, 116, 128, 140, 142
functional behaviour analysis (FBA), 91
functions of behaviour, 88, 91

Gibbs, C, 100
golden questions, 141
greeting rituals, 107-109

Heath, C & D, 58
Heen, S, 49
Herndon, J, 51
Horvath, JC, 119
humour, 134

I statements, 34-35
identifying mood, 108
IDID protocol, 31-32
imperative instruction, 48-49
impromptu conference, 73
inappropriate time, 28-29
individual progress checks in, 18, 65
individual reminders, 22
interleaved practice, 138

intervention, 12
interventions, 97-100
intervention scripts 25-36
inverted models, 155-156
invisible commands, 23
Iovanonne, R, 91

Knight, J, 142-143
Kerbey, L, 43

language, 45-49, 63-64
learning characteristics, 97-989
learning games, 134, 149-160
learning intention, 125-127
learning pit, 119-120, 160
Lemov, D, 20, 106, 109
Lewis, R, 20-21, 31-32, 63, 73, 75-76
limits, 48-49
line debate, 151-152
low-demand environment, 38
low-demand instruction, 37-49
low-key interventions, 11-23

Mackay, J, 34-35, 53, 66
making connection, 108
McREL International, 98
measuring student engagement, 142-144
micro command, 28-30
micro signals, 19-20
mindset, 5, 13-14, 80, 93, 119-120
mistaken goal prompts, 59, 70-73
mistakes, 2, 69
model answers, 141
motivating students, 116
Murphy, L, 40, 43

no, 43-44
no put-downs, 29-30
non-attributive feedback, 23, 32
non-directives, 23
non-verbal commands, 19-20, 46
not here and not now, 29, 56
not negotiable, 29, 49, 56
nudging, 12, 20, 61

observation prompts, 22-23
observing, 40-41
on-task praise, 13-15, 18, 20, 107
one-on-one discussions, 63-64, 66-67
open responses, 70-72
opportunity, 42-43

parallel cueing, 15
partial agreement, 52-5, 58
patterns of student argument, 60
pause time, 74, 141-142
Pentland, A, 21, 132-133
persona, 133
personal connections, 133-134
personal pronouns 44-45
piquing curiosity, 135
pivot phrases, 52
pivoting, 51-59
policies and procedures, 5
positioning, 14-16
positive behaviour framework, 5
positive group correction, 20
praise, 13-16, 20
private individual correction, 20
procedures and policies, 5
professional learning, 62, 98
progress check, 17-19, 65
prompting reflection, 70
proximity, 14-15
purpose of off-task behaviour, 87-95

qualifiers, 42-43
quality mistakes, 2, 77
questioning, 139-140

race the bell, 134, 153-154
rallying calls, 107, 110-111
recording, 92
redirection, 53-55
refining, 104, 147
reflection, 69-70, 73-74
refocusing, 17-18
reframing, 54-56
rehearse, 52, 106-107
relationship building, 6, 49, 62, 108, 131-135

relationship first, task second, 6, 62
reminding, 20-23
repairing, 73
respectful commands, 27-29
responding, 111
responsibility, 66, 73, 82-83
restorative chat, 73, 76
restorative justice approach, 5, 75-76
rewards, 129
rights and responsibilities reminders, 30
routines, 103-104, 107-113, 136
rule prompts, 30-31

sampling tool, 143
saving face, 66-69
school-level response, 5, 66, 81
seeking support, 79-83
sense words, 40
sense-making activities, 122
signal empathy, 57-58
skill and drill approach, 138
snapshot question, 142
spaced practice, 138
spacing, 14-15
statement of value, 55-56
stimulus seeking behaviour, 87, 89, 91, 138
Stone, D, 49
stressors, 137
strewing, 43
struggle, 119-121
student agency, 42-43
student behaviour, 5, 28, 35, 51-52, 71, 88, 146
student engagement, 115-144
student motivation, 115
success criteria, 18, 42, 123-127
symptoms, 88, 97

table tapping, 20
talking it out, 61-77
tantrums 37-38
targeting, 48-49
task review, 118
teacher intervention, 3, 33, 159

Teacher Learning Network, 98, 161
temporary redirection, 55
thirty-second script, 31
Thorsborne, M, 73–75
threshold strategy, 109
time on task tool, 142–143
time-poor, 2
Tomlinson, CA, 121–123
toolkit of strategies, 2, 5
transitions and procedures, 103–113
trial and error process, 2, 59
triggers, 49, 92, 132
Truman, C, 41, 49
trust, 132
turn and talk time, 140–141, 152
typecasting students,

understanding, 21, 89, 119, 135

verbal bullying, 29
Vinegrad, D, 73–75

wait time, 46–47, 140–141
whiteboard relay, 134, 157–158
why, 87–88
wording, 45–46
wondering, 41–42

www.ingramcontent.com/pod-product-compliance
Lightning Source LLC
Chambersburg PA
CBHW052133110526
44591CB00012B/1704